THE

25

Most Dangerous Sales Myths

(and How to Avoid Them)

by

STEPHAN SCHIFFMAN

America's #1 Corporate Sales Trainer

Adams Media
Avon, Massachusetts

Published by Adams Media, a division of F+W Corporation
57 Littlefield Street, Avon, MA 02322 U.S.A.
www.adamsmedia.com

ISBN: 1-59337-014-8

Printed in Canada.

J I H G F E D C B A

Library of Congress Cataloging-in-Publication Data
Schiffman, Stephan.
The 25 most dangerous sales myths / Stephan Schiffman.
p.   cm.
ISBN 1-59337-014-8
1 . Selling—Handbooks, manuals, etc. I. Title: Twenty five most
dangerous sales myths. II. Title.

HF5438.25.S3323 2004
658.85—dc22
2003022383

This publication is designed to provide accurate and authoritative
information with regard to the subject matter covered. It is sold with
the understanding that the publisher is not engaged in rendering legal,
accounting, or other professional advice. If legal advice or other
expert assistance is required, the services of a competent professional
person should be sought.
— From a *Declaration of Principles* jointly adopted by a Committee of the
American Bar Association and a Committee of Publishers and Associations

Many of the designations used by manufacturers and sellers to distin-
guish their products are claimed as trademarks. Where those designations appear in this book and Adams Media was aware of a trademark
claim, the designations have been printed with initial capital letters.

Rear cover photograph:
The Ira Rosen Studios, South Bellmore, New York

This book is available at quantity discounts for bulk purchases.
For information, call 1-800-872-5627.

Contents

Introduction

This book is dedicated to unmasking the most damaging lies, misconceptions, half-truths, "urban legends," and tall tales that have been associated with the world of selling over the last half-century.

Sales Myths Cost You Money

Each of the unfortunate myths, misconceptions, and unwarranted assumptions discussed in this book costs salespeople real-world dollars in annual commissions, year in and year out. My goal here is to make sure that you are not one of those salespeople.

I hope that in setting the record straight with this book, I will be able to help you avoid the most common and dangerous myths about selling . . . and, at the same time, develop the routines and strategies that will put you in front of more of the right people at the right time than you're currently seeing.

Here's hoping you enjoy what follows. It's intended to be both a serious examination of potentially expensive selling errors, and an amusing look at some of the extremely strange things people have managed to convince themselves that they're supposed to believe about business and sales.

Please contact me with your questions, comments, or suggestions about the book—and about any additional myths that you think I may have missed. My e-mail address is *contactus@ dei-sales.com,* and the direct line at D.E.I. Management Group is 1-800-224-2140.

Stephan Schiffman

Acknowledgments

My thanks go out to Brandon Toropov, and, as always, to Anne, Daniele, and Jennifer.

Myth #1:

"Always Be Closing"

"What's my name? [Expletive deleted]! That's my name! You know why? Because you drove a Hyundai to get here, and I drove an $80,000 BMW. THAT'S my name . . . A-B-C—Always Be Closing. Always Be Closing. ALWAYS BE CLOSING!"
  —from David Mamet's *Glengarry Glen Ross*

THE MYTH: You can succeed in sales by focusing obsessively on devoting all of your time, energy, and attention on closing the deal—regardless of the state of your relationship with the prospect or customer.

This may well be the most dangerous myth of them all—so I'm addressing it in the very first chapter.

You still hear a lot of self-appointed sales "experts" promoting the "Always Be Closing" philosophy. (There's even a full-fledged sales training course you can take that goes by this name.)

The idea these trainers and writers usually promote—with enthusiasm—usually revolves around the notion that salespeople should focus their efforts on closing from the earliest possible moment of the relationship, and keep doing so as long as they possibly can.

Here's a selling model that one of the "Always Be Closing" proponents advocates. According to this consultant, this is what the progression of the ideal sale supposedly looks like:

The (So-Called) "ABC" Sales Model
1. Approach
2. Analysis
3. Active Presentation
4. Answer Objections
5. ABC: Always Be Closing

Do you notice anything missing in this sequence?

There's no stage at which we ask the other person anything about what's actually happening in his or her world! There's no point at which we ask, "What's the main thing you're trying to make happen here?" There's no place for us to say, "Tell me something—what have you done to deal with this problem in the past?"

Look at the sequence closely once again. Approach leads directly to analysis, which leads directly to active presentation, which leads directly to answering objections, which leads directly to "always be closing."

Who's doing the approaching? The sales-person, of course.

Who's doing the analyzing? Nine times out of 10, the sales "expert" will tell you that it's not the prospective customer; it's the salesperson. (Notice that analysis isn't information gathering—it's evaluation of what the salesperson believes the circumstances to be, probably based on his or her own existing predispositions and assumptions.)

Who delivers the active presentation? You guessed it, the salesperson.

Who "answers" the "objections"? (These are, truth be told, much more likely to be intuitive negative responses than reasoned, logically sound objections to what's being proposed.) Well, it sure isn't the prospect who deals with negative responses; so it's got to be the salesperson.

And that brings us to the final item, the ABC item: Who's always—and the key word there is "always"—looking for a way to close the deal right away? Why, it's the salesperson.

In this model, there's absolutely no step devoted to finding out what's important from the other person's point of view, for posing questions that show you what his or her priorities are. In fact, if for some reason the prospect wanted to *volunteer* relevant information to the salesperson, there's no step in the sales process to accommodate that! The guiding idea, in other words, is "Always Be Closing" throughout.

All too often, salespeople adopt an "Always Be Closing" attitude because they believe that selling is simply a numbers game. (See Myth #16.) They tell themselves that this approach will work at least part of the time, and they're right. Everything works at least part of the time. So they ask themselves, "What's the worst that could happen?"

Here's what is likely to happen if you make "Always Be Closing" a way of life:

• People won't give you good information. (They will, very often, tell you whatever they think is most likely to make you go away.)

• People won't tell you the truth. (They're far more likely to say things like, "I have to talk to my boss about this," when they have no intention of doing any such thing.)

• People won't give you referrals. (They're afraid you'll pull the same "Always Be Closing" techniques on their colleagues or friends.)

• People won't listen to what you have to say (because you haven't listened to what they have to say).

• People won't trust you. (Why should they?)

• When people do buy from you—because you happened to connect with them while they were in active "search" mode—they'll be statistically unlikely to build a meaningful business partnership with you. (In other words, when someone comes along with a better deal, your customer will bolt. There's no loyalty and no long-term relationship.)

In practical terms, "Always Be Closing" translates as: "Ask for the business at every possible opportunity, regardless of how much—or how little—unique information you've gathered from the other person." All the entertaining macho posturing aside, this is a truly unfortunate foundation for any sales career.

Even though a number of sales "experts" claim that closing all the time isn't what they mean when they promote the "Always Be Closing" model, it's hard to see what they are promoting. The reality is that "close, close, close" is precisely how most salespeople understand—and apply—this selling principle. If you doubt this, listen closely to the next telemarketing call you receive and see whether it fits the pattern I've described.

For reasons that have, I hope, become clear to you by now, "Always Be Closing" is a fatally flawed sales philosophy.

We'll be exploring an effective alternative to it in the next chapter.

THE REALITY: Steer clear of the "Always Be Closing" selling philosophy.

Selling Requires "Can't-Miss" Closing Tricks

"Which of these would you prefer—the blue model or the red model?"
> —The classic "preference close," praised by hundreds of sales trainers over the years. The prospect is supposed to forget that he hasn't yet decided whether it makes sense to buy anything, and focus instead on whether what he doesn't yet want to buy should be red or blue.

THE MYTH: You can build long-term relationships with silly closing strategies.

Did you ever see the segment on David Letterman's television show entitled "Stupid Human Tricks"?

Ordinary, everyday people come up on stage to show off their unusual performing talents. If you've ever played the piano with your hands tied behind your back, balanced a 16-foot canoe on your chin, or stopped a ceiling fan with your head—stop and think for a moment. Did you do these things on national television, in front of millions of people? If so, then you are almost certainly a participant in Letterman's "Stupid Human Tricks" segment. If not, don't despair: There's still time to find your special ability, contact Dave, and win a chance to humiliate yourself in front of a global viewing audience.

These unique "Stupid Human Tricks" talents are hard to ignore, but they have, I would argue, very little practical application in everyday life. They remind me of a very similar category of activity I like to call "Stupid Closing Tricks."

Below, you will find some variations on real-life examples of "Stupid Closing Tricks" that have been advocated by some supposed expert or other. Each is, I would argue, an expression of the misguided "Always Be Closing" philosophy (see Myth #1), which places a premium on pressuring the customer from the moment the relationship begins, and which relegates information-gathering to a low, or nonexistent, place on the priority list.

• After reviewing all the possible benefits of your product or service, look the prospect in the eye and say: "You've seen what ABC widgets have to offer, and I know you know what their value is. Heck, a half-blind chimpanzee could see that. So why don't you sign up?"

• If your prospect is male and married, say, "Listen—I know you would have bought two of our widgets for your wife when you first fell in love with her. You love her at least half as much now, don't you? Come on, Mr. Prospect, sign up."

• Put your arm around the prospect's shoulder and say, "Mr. Prospect, I just want to tell you something—as one man to another. If I had the same challenges you had, and if I faced the same obstacles you do right now, there is absolutely nothing in the world that would keep me from signing up. What do you say?"

• If you know the prospect has a family and cares about them, say, "Mr. Prospect, if you don't want to place an order for our widgets for yourself, you should at least give this a try for your family's sake. Remember, they rely on you, just like my wife and children rely on me. It's their future that's at stake, isn't it? Well, then, why don't you sign on, for them?"

• If the prospect reacts negatively to any attempt to close, say, "Mr. Prospect, you may feel like I've been a little pushy with you today—and you know what? I have. And let me tell you why I've been pushy. It's because our widgets really are the highest-quality widgets on the market. If that weren't true, I guarantee you that I wouldn't be putting any pressure on you. Listen, I have a wife and kids just like you do, and believe me, I want them to feel great about me, just like you want your family to be proud of you. All I'm asking you to do is what X thousand others have done, and sign on with us so you can experience their quality for yourself. What do you say?"

• Here's one that I came across online; it's supposed to be used in the personal training industry. Let's say you're the prospect. When you sign up for one of those free-week-at-the-gym offers, the gym's objective is, of course, to get you to buy a long-term membership. If you decline all the gym's hard-sell efforts to "go in for the kill" and get you to sign up, as the experts like to say, guess what the salesperson is supposed to do? Pull out a box of doughnuts, slam them on the table in front of you, look you in the eye, and say, "All right, then—go ahead. Give up. And you might as well take these with you."

• And finally—this is one of my favorites—*match the prospect's physical movements* in order to show your commonality. Supposedly, if you do the "mirror" exercise with your contact during your meeting, this practice convinces him or her that you're really a kindred spirit . . . and magically turns a skeptical contact into a customer.

Again—*people really teach this stuff.* Today. In the twenty-first century. Wouldn't you agree that these all sound like pretty absurd pieces of "selling advice"?

I won't even try to tell you about the more exotic—but equally stupid—strategies that go by special names, like the Ben Franklin close, the Roll-the-Pen close, the Puppy Dog close, and so on. Suffice to say . . . I've heard it all.

All these various closing tricks—and hundreds more just as outlandish—really aren't what you want to spend your time memorizing. There's a much simpler, and much more effective, closing strategy you can use. It's the best alternative to "Stupid Closing Tricks" I've ever come across. It sounds like this:

"Mr. Prospect—it makes sense to me. What do you think?"

In order for that technique to work, though, you have to be willing to do some work ahead of time—by working with the prospect to find out whether or not what you're suggesting really does make sense.

You'll get some ideas on how to do that in some of the later chapters of this book. For now, I want you to ask yourself: Which closing technique would you rather say out loud to a prospect? The one that asks him whether or not what you've proposed makes sense? Or the one that compares him to a half-blind chimpanzee?

THE REALITY: Don't bother trying to memorize "can't-miss" closing tricks.

Myth #3:

You Can "Warm Up" Your Cold Call with Mysterious Packages

"The discovery of a mysterious package on Tuesday morning sparked the evacuation of about 30 people from nearby homes and businesses and forced the declaration of a hazardous substance emergency."
—Recent news item from New Zealand. Is this really how you want to start your business relationships?

THE MYTH: Sending packages containing strange objects helps you to open up the sales relationship.

Over the years, I've read about dozens of "send an unusual package" schemes that various salespeople and sales managers have come up with. Most are designed to get you onto the person's "radar screen" by means of a cumbersome box that contains some unusual object. Some of these plans are inventive—but none of them, in my book, are preferable to a well-structured, confidently delivered phone call suggesting a meeting at a specific place and time.

I've heard stories of people who send a strange oblong box to the decision-maker. When the recipient opens the box, he or she finds a single shoe, accompanied by a small note bearing some variation on the message, "Now that I've got my foot in the door . . . " (One can only hope that a new, clean shoe is used.)

I also heard a story of a fellow who wanted to contact the general manager of a radio station. This enterprising person sent his target person a package with a small rubber ball. Progressively larger . . . um . . . spheres were sent on subsequent days for a week. Finally, the target person got a huge box, containing a massive . . . um . . . sphere. The message, if I recall correctly, was revealed in the note that accompanied this chair-sized box. The sender wanted the recipient to know that he possessed large enough . . . um . . . spheres to justify a face-to-face meeting. Now, when the sender makes his call to set up the meeting, what kind of reaction do you honestly think he is going to get?

I even met someone once who had been sent a free pair of socks in the mail by a salesperson! No, the salesperson wasn't selling socks. I never learned what point he was trying to make, and I doubt it made any kind of positive impression on anyone at the target organization, either. How long do you really pay attention to something like that? A moment or two. Then you're back to whatever you were doing before you opened the odd package.

Maybe you're even a little resentful about the time and attention you spent trying to figure out why on earth someone would mail you a box with a pair of socks in it.

I've heard about people sending horror movie props, toys, fruit baskets, and all manner of attention-getting devices to people with whom they wanted to develop business relationships. The idea seems to be that this send-a-package approach will leave the recipient with an unforgettable impression once the sender actually picks up the phone and tries to make contact.

There will be an impression, all right. But I'm not so sure it's the impression you'd want to use as the beginning of a successful business relationship.

All of these "send a strange package" strategies, no matter how inventive, send a single, unstated, but ultimately dangerous message from the salesperson to the decision-maker: "I'm actually afraid to call you . . . and I'm sending along this object so the call will eventually go a little easier than it otherwise might."

Is there really any good reason to start out the business relationship by confirming to the other person that we're afraid of connecting with him or her in a more traditional manner? What else, the contact may wonder, are we likely to be afraid of?

Here's my advice: Don't send strange messenger deliveries, single shoes, progressively larger spheres, or anything else out of the ordinary before connecting with a prospect by phone. Don't under-estimate the possibility that your unusual package may go unopened. (These are security-minded times in which we live, after all.) And by all means, avoid sending packages that may call into question your taste or professionalism.

Mystery packages may well do your cause more harm than good. You'll run the risk of coming off as someone who's frightened of a central component of the salesperson's job—namely, reaching out and making contact with sales prospects.

There's no reason to be afraid of that. Pick up the phone and make the call. Ask directly and without apology for a face-to-face appointment.

(You'll find plenty of proven, tested strategies for securing appointments by phone in my book *Cold Calling Techniques (That Really Work)*; you can also visit my Web site for prospecting ideas: *www.dei-sales.com*.)

THE REALITY: Don't risk sending the wrong message by sending a mysterious package.

Myth #4:

Sending Strange Business Letters Works

"Dear Mr. ____ : Don't read this unless you're interested in saving your company $100,000 per year."
— Lead sentence of a "creative" sales letter

THE MYTH: Prospects love bizarre letters from strangers.

"Make Your Point with Fake Money!" That was the advice that appeared in one of the nation's leading sales newsletters recently. The article offered a case study profiling a "creative idea" that a Florida consultant tried out on her prospects.

This consultant, we read, had estimated that she could save a certain business approximately $30,000 a year. She apparently had had trouble getting in touch with the contact she wanted to work with, so in order to "knock down the prospect's resistance," she came up with an ingenious scheme to get the appointment. She sent $540 in fake money to the contact, along with a note upbraiding him for ignoring the opportunity to take advantage of this much extra cash every week. She closed the letter by ordering him to call her when he was eager "to make this money real."

This is a variation on the "mystery package" idea, and it's just as silly. (It's a little cheaper, but it's just as silly.)

There are probably hundreds of "send a strange letter" sales tricks. Some of them, like this one, ask you to send props or bogus "documents." Others ask you to develop a wacky headline and put it in huge type. None of these tricks, I believe, is a wise investment of your time. The question is not whether such techniques *ever* work—everything will work *eventually* if you try it on a large enough sample of people. The question is whether you should build your daily selling routine around such stunts.

Again: You'll get a much higher rate of return—and lay a better foundation for any meetings you actually schedule—by reaching out to the person by means of a voice-to-voice phone call or a concise, confidently delivered voice-mail message. (By the way, you'll learn how to leave a powerful voice-mail message in Myth #11.)

THE REALITY: Save the fake money for your next game of Monopoly.

People Love It When You Pretend You're Not a Salesperson

"O, what a tangled web we weave,
When first we practice to deceive."
—Sir Walter Scott

THE MYTH: Lying about who you are is a great way to launch a relationship with someone.

"You've won a prize!"
"I'm conducting a survey for my organization."
"This is just a service call . . . but listen, as long as I've got you on the line . . . "

Fifty years ago, sales managers would tell their salespeople to use these kinds of silly and misleading opening lines on their prospects. Amazingly, you still run into people who instruct sales teams to use these or similar lines on people they call or meet. Some supervisors write carefully crafted scripts to make sure that the lies or misstatements are delivered with verbatim precision.

We've all gotten manipulative, misleading appeals like this from salespeople from time to time. And I think it's fair to say we've all resented those appeals.

There's really no reason to pretend to be anybody other than who you really are when you reach out to people, either on the phone or in person. I'm actually quite proud of what I do for a living, and I hope you're proud of what you do. I don't have any reservations about telling people *exactly* what my company does and what my role is. To tell you the truth, I tell people what I do at every conceivable opportunity. Maybe I do bring my company into the conversation a little too much . . . but that habit is, I would argue, far better than misleading people about what I actually do. The big problem with starting a call or a meeting with a misleading statement is that it *destroys credibility with the other person* . . . and that's very difficult to repair.

So be up-front with the people you come in contact with. Say who you are, what you do, what your company does, and what you'd like to see happen next in the relationship. You'll get much further than you ever would by pretending to be arranging for the delivery of a prize, or conducting a survey, or making some kind of maintenance call.

THE REALITY: Tell the truth. It's easier to remember.

MYTH #6:

Decision-Makers Adore Unannounced Visitors

"I really don't like people who show up unannounced."

—From an old campfire tale

THE MYTH: Materializing unannounced at a stranger's office and demanding a face-to-face meeting is the best way to win friends and influence people.

Do you remember the movie *Wall Street*? In that film, Michael Douglas plays an investment tycoon, and Charlie Sheen plays a young salesperson eager to climb the ladder of success to the highest possible level. To launch a relationship with Douglas, Sheen shows up without an appointment in the older man's office—bearing a gift. (He's learned that it's Douglas's birthday.)

When Douglas discovers his unexpected visitor, he's only slightly annoyed—and he's more than a little impressed. He's got enough respect for the salesperson's chutzpah to grant him a face-to-face meeting . . . and Sheen's eventful career in finance is launched.

That's the movies.

In real life, decision-makers *loathe* unannounced visitors, whether or not they do research ahead of time or come bearing gifts. I'm not saying that there aren't industries in which salespeople drop by office parks and corporate headquarters unannounced and eventually close sales, and I'm certainly not saying that no one will ever meet with you if you wander from reception area to reception area. What I am saying is that time is precious, and you should think long and hard before you spend your day driving all around your territory with a car full of gifts for decision-makers you haven't met yet.

I've mentioned before that the most effective way of establishing contact with businesspeople you hope to meet in person is by means of a prospecting telephone call. Here's an example of what such a call should sound like.

Attention statement: Hello, Mr. Jones.
Identification statement: This is Mike Smith from ABC Company. I don't know whether you've ever heard of us—we're the largest producer of widgets on the Eastern seaboard.
Reason for the call: The reason I'm calling you specifically today is that we just completed a program for Acme Manufacturing that helped them to

improve productivity by 15 percent in one quarter. I'd love to get together with you to show you the program we put together for Acme—can we meet on January 16th at 3:00?

THEN STOP TALKING. You don't have to use my words, but you do have to use a *standardized* script, one that you know backwards and forwards and can deliver in exactly the same way, each and every time you call to try to set up an appointment.

Don't get too hung up about "qualifying" leads before you call them to ask for an appointment. Ask directly for a specific time and date for the meeting during your cold call. Avoid extended conversations during prospecting calls. If the goal of the call is simply to set an appointment, then a lengthy call is a bad sign. The person is probably either screening you or giving you abuse.

My guess is that if you practice a simple script like the one I've just shared with you for just a few hours, learn a few basic turnarounds (visit *www.dei-sales.com* to learn more about turning around initial negative responses), and then make it your goal to speak to, say, 20 decision-makers a day, you'll have all the first meetings you need.

What's more, you won't have to worry about the receptionist eyeing your gift-wrapped package warily, calling security on you, or looking at you as though you're an escapee from a lunatic asylum.

THE REALITY: Call first.

MYTH #7:

Price Always Carries the Day

"Selling on price is not really selling at all."
—John Carroll

THE MYTH: Price is the most important factor in selling.

"They beat the pants off of us on price—we didn't have a chance."

"Of course they got the deal! Their pricing structure is a lot more attractive than ours is."

"We're just going to have to face it; we're never going to be competitive in this industry until we find some way to lower our prices."

To hear most salespeople talk, you'd suspect that there is no sales barrier so impossible to overcome as a lower price offered by a competitor. But the Dayton, Ohio–based H.R. Chally Group, a nationally respected sales force benchmarking firm with whom I've worked many times, conducted a fascinating poll of more than 15,000 business customers to find out what the most important factors were for satisfaction in a business relationship with a vendor. Their results suggest that price may not be the be-all and end-all for salespeople after all.

There are four critical factors for maintaining a satisfactory relationship with a vendor, according to H.R. Chally. The four are reproduced below; to arrive at their numerical distributions, Chally compared poll responses with actual purchase decisions, and correlated the two.

Critical Factors in Selecting a Vendor
- The salesperson's competence (contributes 39 percent to overall satisfaction).
- The total customer solution (contributes 22 percent to overall satisfaction).
- The quality of the product or service (contributes 21 percent to overall satisfaction).
- A competitive price (contributes only 18 percent to overall satisfaction).

Notice that, while price is a factor, it is the *least important* of the four uncovered by the Chally poll. Notice, too, that the salesperson's ability to service the account (and, presumably, implement the plan he or she developed for the customer) is roughly twice as important as price.

Especially in those situations where the features of your product offering are roughly equivalent to those of your competition, the Chally results are revealing. They suggest that your own commitment to the relationship with the prospect or customer—as well as your ability to match what your company offers to what the prospect or customer does—will be what determines the quality and longevity of the relationship.

The "price always carries the day" myth is, perhaps, one of those myths that salespeople repeat to themselves until they believe that it's true. It often causes salespeople to focus their efforts on winning pricing concessions from management. This is a shame, because they should be focusing their efforts on how to implement, to the highest possible standards, the plans they've developed for the customers they already have.

THE REALITY: Build relationships—not just discounts.

MYTH #8:

Selling Effectively Means "Trapping" the Prospect

"Ever get the feeling you've been cheated?"
—John Lydon

THE MYTH: Closing means entrapment.

There is a theory, widely circulated in the sales training industry, that selling is like a box, and closing a sale is like slamming the door of that box shut so as to "trap" the prospective customer.

I did not make this metaphor up. It is a popular image in the world of sales. The "trap door" in this selling model is supposedly the salesperson's enthusiasm. That, we are told, is what is "closing."

The box, in one version, has a number of sides, each of which is labeled to represent things like sincerity, trust, product knowledge, and so on. The salesperson's energy and enthusiasm, supposedly, are what traps the prospect and finalizes the deal. Nowhere on the box diagram with the little trap door, however, does one find a label for "finding out what makes sense to the other person" or "sharing relevant success stories." These are what will actually make the most difference in your interactions with prospective customers—and what will, in the long run, make success as a salesperson possible.

Matching up what the other person is doing now with what you've done with other satisfied customers may not be a lot like a swinging trap door, but it is the best way to win customers over time.

Instead of planning out how to "trap" your prospect, use the time for a more constructive purpose. Memorize at least six specific success stories about your company. The more success stories you have, the more likely you are able to appeal to one that's a "perfect fit" when talking to a prospect or customer. (Six, I would argue, is a bare minimum; a dozen would be an ideal number for a relatively new salesperson, I think.)

No amount of enthusiasm can conceal an inability to discuss what your company actually has accomplished. Knowing exactly how your organization has helped your customers in the past is essential. You must be able to talk persuasively about these experiences during a sales meeting, and draw relevant parallels between what the prospect is facing and a problem that a client or customer faced earlier. Fancy proposals and outlines are nice, but your prospects want to know *why* they should do business with you. Be sure you can intelligently discuss the successes you or your organization have been able to deliver to others. If you can build hard figures into your success stories—something the prospect can measure and compare to his or her own world—so much the better.

If you don't know between six and 12 success stories about your business, you probably shouldn't even go out on a first appointment with a prospective customer! And it should go without saying that, without this ability to share practical knowledge about how your company has helped other people, any attempt to "trap" the other person is futile.

THE REALITY: Do the homework. Talk to your colleagues. Talk to your supervisor. Get the details about when, where, and how your company has added value. Be ready to share those details when the opportunity arises. And forget about trying to "trap" the prospect.

Never Ask a Question When You Don't Know What the Answer Will Be

"Too much certainty can be problematic."
—Arthur Conan Doyle

THE MYTH: Only ask questions that allow you to "control the conversation."

This myth encourages us to fall into the "salesperson-as-prosecuting-attorney" trap.

There are many sales managers and sales trainers who take the idea of "controlling" a face-to-face meeting to such absurd lengths that they actually advocate adopting this principle. Ask a question that you can't guess the likely answer to, they warn, and you risk looking foolish in front of the prospect, displaying gaps in your product or industry knowledge, or (heaven help us) losing "control" of the meeting.

Here's a news flash: Only recommendations

that make sense to the prospect are *right* from his or her point of view. And the only way for us to be *right* is to get *righted*. That means we have to let the prospect correct us.

If you're "controlling" the meeting by reciting a list of predetermined questions—the same questions at every meeting with every prospect—that's too much "control" of the meeting. You'll get further with your prospects, and build better relationships, if you ask *big questions that you don't know the answers to* (such as, "What made you decide to call us?") and then follow the answers wherever they lead.

Plenty of salespeople go on "autopilot" during meetings with prospects by focusing only on the questions they think they know the answers to! All too often, the "questions" these salespeople ask during meetings with prospects are little more than excuses for delivering long monologues about their product or service. I think this happens because a meeting with a prospect is usually perceived as a stressful situation, and when we feel stress, we tend to fall back on what's familiar to us. It's our responsibility, therefore, to become more familiar with the questions we want to ask than we are with the product or service we sell! (Otherwise, we'll simply "throw up" on the prospect by dumping a lot of information, most of it irrelevant.)

Make a list of 10 questions you would like to

ask each prospect you visit. Review the questions over and over again before your meeting. (But don't use good preparation as an excuse to barrage the person with a "checklist" of questions. Pose a single far-reaching question, then ask effective follow-ups that allow you to follow the other person's lead. Then pose another far-reaching question, and continue the process.)

Following are some examples of good "generic" questions . . . but be sure you prepare company-specific queries as well.

An excellent initial question to ask a prospect is, "I'm just curious, how does someone become a (marketing manager, vice-president of engineering, widget specialist, whatever)?"

Other good questions to ask include these:

- For the early part of the meeting: "I checked our records, and I noticed that you're not currently a customer of ours. Why not?"
- For situations where you called the prospect: "I'm just curious; what were you going to do in such-and-such an area if I hadn't called you?"
- For situations where the prospect called you: "How did you hear about us?"
- For just about any situation: "Just out of curiosity—who have you worked with in the past on projects like this? How did you decide to work with them?"

The "never ask a question you don't know the answer to" principle often keeps salespeople from asking for a Next Step at the conclusion of the first meeting. After all, they don't know whether the other person will say "yes" to their request for a meeting—and they might lose control of the conversation if they ask for another appointment then and there!

Before you conclude the first meeting, ask for the Next Step. Ask for it while you're there. Say, "You know what? You've given me a lot to think about. What I'd like to do is go back to my office, talk this over with a couple of people, and come back here next Tuesday at 2:00 so I can show you an outline of how we might be able to work together. Does that time work?"

Then wait and see what comes back.

This selling principle is simple and easy to implement; it is universally observed by top performing salespeople. I'm not going to spend a lot of time discussing it, because it is, quite frankly, blindingly obvious once you encounter it. Simply make a point of asking for the next meeting at the conclusion of the meeting you're in. Propose a specific time and date; stop talking. See what happens. If you do this at every sales meeting, you'll find out where the contact really stands, you'll spend less time spinning your wheels, and you'll dramatically shorten your sales cycle, typically by between two and four weeks.

Why *wouldn't* you ask that kind of question? Because you don't know the answer to the question? Because it causes you to "lose control" of the meeting? Nonsense! You will lose control of the entire *relationship,* and spend days or weeks working on proposals that turn into nothing, if you don't let the prospect tell you whether or not he or she is interested in moving forward to the next phase of the sales relationship with you. You should only invest your time and attention in people who are willing to invest their time and attention with you, and you're not going to find out who those people are unless you ask them to do something!

You have to ask yourself:

- What's your strategy for keeping forward momentum in the relationship once the meeting ends?
- What will your primary Next Step strategy be?
- What will your backup Next Step strategy be?

Whatever course of action you outline with your prospect, it must be specific, and it must involve some kind of action on the part of the prospect.

Even if you can't get a Next Step with a time and date attached, you can ask for some kind of action from your prospect.

Make a list of things you can ask a prospect to

do if you're unable to get a clear Next Step to discuss working together. Here are some ideas.

If you can't get the prospect to commit to scheduling a meeting or other in-person event—it's not the end of the world! Ask the person to:

- Schedule a date and time for a conference call with your boss to discuss what the future looks like in areas relevant to your product/service.
- Give you his or her opinion on a new marketing initiative.
- Visit your Web site and e-mail you with feedback on its layout and design.
- Subscribe to your online newsletter.
- Critique an article you're writing.
- Help test a new product or service (for free).
- Survey key players' opinions (so you can follow up with a "summary report" that adds value to the person's day).

There are dozens, probably hundreds of things you can ask your contact to do to keep the relationship alive. But you have to take the initiative and ask—even if you're not sure what the response to your question will be!

THE REALITY: Ask prospects big questions and follow the answers wherever they go.

MYTH #10:

Always Try to Outsmart the Buyer

"Never give a sucker an even break."
—W. C. Fields, who was, perhaps, a better
entertainer than a sales manager

THE MYTH: Sales success depends on outfoxing your prospect.

The prospect: ally or adversary?

Just about anyone who's ever purchased a new car has encountered a salesperson whose goal in life was to outsmart the buyer. Nowadays, auto dealerships are busy trying to find ways to send all the right "consumer-friendly" signals—like supposedly "haggle-free" pricing schemes that mask outrageous markups. But the basic dynamics of the relationship are, all too often, totally unchanged: Keep the prospect off-balance, control the dialogue at all costs, and sneak in lots of expensive extras and add-ons while your contact isn't looking.

Auto dealerships may be the most obvious example of this kind of selling, but they're certainly

---

43

not the only examples. Any salesperson, in any industry, can play "outsmart the buyer"—as long as he or she is willing to sacrifice trust, repeat business, and positive word of mouth for short-term gain.

Here are some of the most easy-to-recognize hallmarks of "outsmart-the-buyer" selling:

• *Asking lots of questions—in order to keep the prospect from asking questions of his own.* These kinds of salespeople are most comfortable when they're doing most or all of the talking. That means peppering the prospect with a well-rehearsed series of questions, and never allowing the other person the chance to share meaningful information or raise questions or concerns.

• *Lying about their job situation.* Some of these salespeople will claim that it's their first day on the job in order to win sympathy from the prospective buyer. Some will solemnly inform the most gullible-looking prospects that their job is on the line—if they don't close this sale, their family goes out on the street.

• *Using dubious tactics to control the prospect's physical environment.* Once the environment is under control, the theory, the mind control can begin. Think condo sales: Once they get you to agree to take the "tour," the sales team is in control. Eventually, they get you into the "closing room," and they act like they don't have to let you out unless you ask to speak to your attorney. I've even heard stories of auto salespeople who "park" the prospect's trade-in vehicle at the beginning of the meeting, then have "trouble finding it" when the person announces he's not going to buy. The objective: to win another 20 minutes of "chair time" with you in the salesperson's office.

• *Good cop, bad cop.* Trying to negotiate terms? Some salespeople will actually pull out this ancient interrogation ruse, usually by presenting themselves as the fair-minded empathetic one and their superior as the irrational hothead. The idea is to wear the prospect down and get him to agree to just about anything . . . in exchange for an end to the abuse.

• *The "written in stone" ruse.* See something in the offer or contract you don't like? Too bad for you, because it's "standard boilerplate." Any attempt to change it would bring down the vengeance of the gods.

• *The "let's talk about it later" ruse.* A classic piece of manipulation. Once you've begun trying to hammer out the details of your deal, you'll raise an important issue—say, the payment terms. The salesperson will suggest that the two of you work together to resolve some minor issues first, and then come back to the big stuff once you've built up a little rapport and good faith. The goal here is to *postpone* coming to terms on major questions until the very last possible moment, when the salesperson knows you'll be statistically more likely to grant concessions in order to be done with the whole process. This is particularly common when the prospect is working against some kind of immovable deadline (such as a grand opening or a Web site launch that's been heavily promoted).

Salespeople who try to outsmart the buyer are basically one step—and a very short step, at that—away from con artists. If you want to build trust, respect, and the realistic possibility of repeat business and positive referrals, play it straight with your prospects and customers, and forget about trying to outwit them.

THE REALITY: Don't try to outsmart your prospects and customers.

Long, Detailed, and/or Wacky Voice-Mail Messages Are Great Selling Weapons

"Voice mail is your chance to talk! Start selling!"
—Sales training "expert"

THE MYTH: Some decision-makers will just love getting long or unusual voice-mail messages.

Recently, I read an article that encouraged salespeople to leave detailed, in-depth monologues on the message systems of certain contacts. Supposedly, people who display a slow, measured way of speaking on their outgoing messages are eager to get long-winded messages from total strangers. The message: "Let it all hang out" in your voice-mail messages to these prospects.

This is terrible advice. We've trained more than half a million salespeople and left messages for literally hundreds of thousands of decision-makers as part of our own selling efforts over the years.

We've identified one and only one reliable rule when it comes to the length of the messages you leave on the voice-mail systems of people you haven't spoken to before: *Short and to the point gets better results than long and rambling.*

No matter what kind of speaking style you've detected on the person's outgoing message, you can rest assured that the person has one objective when evaluating voice-mail messages: deleting as many of them as possible. If it takes you forever to get to the point or to supply contact information, you'll be ignored. If you deliver a confident, concise message that makes absolutely clear what you want the other person to do (give you a return call) and how the other person is supposed to do it (by dialing a number that you say twice, very clearly), you will get return calls.

Stay away from the monologues. Keep your messages short and to the point. Here's a message format we use to get a roughly 75 percent return-call rate:

"Jim Prospect—Mike Miller here from ABC Company. I'm calling you regarding Acme Worldwide. Please give me a call back at 212/555-1212. That's 212/555-1212. I look forward to hearing from you!"

Would *you* return that call? I would.
No long, drawn-out explanations—just the

essentials. In this case, "Acme Worldwide" is a company we've worked with before—one that the person we're calling will recognize.

When we get the call back, we'll say something like this:

> "Thanks for giving me a call back, Jim—and let me tell you why I called you about Acme Worldwide. I'm not sure if you're familiar with my company, ABC, but we are a widget-refinishing firm that's been in business for over 40 years. Acme is one of our clients—we just completed a program with them that helped them to lower their widget costs by 30 percent. The reason I'm calling you specifically is that I'd like to come by and show you the plan we put together for Acme. Can we meet this Tuesday at 2:00?"

Now, if you were to put all of that into the initial voice-mail message, you'd almost certainly get your message deleted. If, on the other hand, you were to use the concise initial message I've outlined, and *then* deliver your calling approach, you'd be much more likely to get the appointment.

The only exception to this principle is the situation where you have been trading phone messages for some time with someone who apparently does want to talk to you. In that situation, when you've got a week or so of "phone tag" under your belt, it is perfectly acceptable to suggest in a brief message that you drop by at a certain date and time and see what happens.

This kind of message might sound something like this:

> "Jim, we missed each other this morning, but I just wanted to follow up on our last discussion and see whether it made sense for me to come by on October 29 at 10:00 to show you what we did for ABC Company. Can I meet with you then? Please let me know. I'm at 978/555-1212."

What if there's no response? That means this is not a real prospect. What if there's an instantaneous response along the lines of, "No—please don't come"? Then you are definitely not looking at a real prospect. What if there's a response along the lines of, "I can't make it at 10:00—let's meet at 2:00 instead"? Congratulations: You've got a Next Step—and a prospect.

Our goal throughout the sales process is to suggest forward movement in the relationship by delivering concise messages that elicit a reaction from the other person. Our prospecting calls should do this; our in-person meetings should do this; our presentations should do this. Shouldn't our voice-mail messages do this, as well?

Another way to do this through voice mail is to have *your manager* call an "on-the-fence" prospect and leave a message saying, "I understand we're going to be doing business together!" That will definitely produce a reaction. Too "pushy"? I don't think so. When your manager gets a call back, positive or negative, you'll have a better sense of exactly where you stand with the person. And the call may uncover information that would otherwise have remained concealed.

Leave a *short* message—not your whole calling script or full-scale sales pitch. This kind of message will be much more likely to get a response from the other person. That's the reason you're placing the call in the first place, right?

THE REALITY: Keep voice-mail messages short, sweet, and to the point.

E-Mail Is Replacing the Telephone as a Sales Tool

"If it's spam, the message is 'delete.'"
—*CNET.com Tech News*

THE MYTH: Prospecting by phone is becoming passé in the age of e-mail.

Every once in a while, you'll come across an article or lecture from someone who claims that you can use e-mail messages to total strangers as your primary prospecting tool. Some articles even suggest that e-mail appeals have completely replaced business phone calls, including sales calls, because people supposedly "prefer" communicating by e-mail these days.

I don't buy these claims, for two reasons: First and foremost, people get so much junk e-mail these days that they don't have time to bother with messages from people they don't recognize. And second, people are so worried about getting a dangerous computer virus that a large number of them will probably avoid opening an unfamiliar e-mail message, even if they do have the time or inclination to do so. (The odds of getting your message noticed or opened tend to drop, predictably, if you're sending an attachment to someone you don't know.)

If we hope to make anything meaningful happen in sales, we must get in the habit of doing something deliberate, something impossible to ignore—something that all but forces the other person to respond to us. The people who then *do* respond to us are our *prospects*; they're the ones we should focus our attention on. E-mail is, as a general rule, a pretty lousy tool for delivering impossible-to-ignore messages about setting first appointments. E-mail can, however, help us to initiate action with current customers and *some* prospects—namely, those who already know who we are.

Here are some examples of effective use of e-mail on the sales front.

Follow through on your face-to-face meetings. In addition to sending a written note, send a brief (one- to five-line) e-mail thanking your contact for his or her time. Mention the person's name in the header. In the body of the text, reinforce the time and date of whatever Next Step you have established—be it a meeting, a phone conference, a tour of a plant, attendance at an industry event, or any other agreed-upon contact. Be sure to personalize your message. ("I'm looking forward to speaking further with you about _____ when we meet on Tuesday.")

Offer brief status reports on current initiatives. If you've promised to check into a problem, gather information from a group of people, or develop a new strategy to meet a prospect's goals, you can use e-mail to keep your contact up to date on what's going on. Don't send reports every day (unless you've been asked to do so); don't overwhelm the person with information. Just keep an ongoing dialogue going: "As you requested, I spoke with the following members of your team today . . . " Then reinforce the date and time of your next contact with the person you're e-mailing.

Deliver value *after* the sale. Keep in touch with current customers by e-mailing them *relevant* strategies on how to implement or get the best results from what you've sold them. Make sure your messages are targeted to the right people . . . and make sure what you send doesn't sound like "spam" (mass advertising forwarded by e-mail). Electronic versions of your company newsletter may be helpful to your customers. Perhaps even more effective—and targeted—are e-mails that point your contact toward a relevant article or Web site you've found that seems to match his or her business interests. In these situations, the "covering" message should be as concise as possible. ("I thought you'd find the attached article of interest, given what we discussed on Wednesday about your division's sales targets.") A day or so later, you can then follow up on these e-mails with a casual phone call—"What did you think of the article I sent along?"—and, if you wish, arrange a face-to-face meeting to discuss long-term goals and objectives.

Say, "I was thinking we ought to get together." Often, a short e-mail message like this, with a date and time for a proposed meeting, will help you re-establish contact with someone you have made some kind of contact with in the past, but who has not been returning phone messages. Consider using this strategy for people who bought from you in the past, but have simply fallen out of the loop.

However you decide to use e-mail, be sure to keep your messages direct and to the point, and to follow basic rules of online etiquette. (For instance: Don't adopt an overly familiar tone or use inappropriate humor; don't type your message with the CAPS LOCK key on.)

THE REALITY: Use e-mail appropriately—and don't rely on it as a prospecting tool.

MYTH #13:

Fight, Fight, Fight When You Hear Negative Responses!

"Apply enough pressure to get the customer to buy when he says, 'I'm not sold.'"
—Overheard at a sales training seminar

THE MYTH: Might makes right when it comes to handling objections.

Fight 'em! Pressure 'em! Overpower 'em!

That's the advice many hard-sell sales "experts" will still give you about dealing with negative responses. It's also, by all appearances, the advice that most salespeople follow when they encounter resistance from their prospects. Sometimes I wonder: Is sales really a job best suited to those whose aim is to get as much conflict as possible into their work day? I'm sometimes tempted to answer "yes," based on some of the calls I receive from salespeople.

Here's a "dialogue of the deaf" based on a call I received recently.

Salesperson: I'd like to meet with you so I can show you . . .

Decision-Maker: I'm really not interested in talking about any of that with you.

Salesperson: Not *interested*? How could you possibly not be *interested* when I haven't even told you what I want to meet with you about? What exactly aren't you interested in, if I may ask?

Decision-Maker: Look. I told you—I'm not interested in meeting with you, okay?

Salesperson: Excuse me—you said, "I'm not interested in talking about *any of that*." And you said, quote, "any of that," unquote, *before* I told you a single, solitary word about the purpose of the meeting I was proposing. Now would you kindly inform me what, specifically, you meant when you said the words "any of that"? I'm not sure what you were getting at.

Decision-Maker: (Hangs up.)

This dead-end calling approach is basically a variation on the closing techniques that attempt to embarrass the prospect into buying from you. ("Mr. Jones, do you mean to tell me, right here in front of your own kids, that you don't earn enough money to ensure that they have access to a quality set of encyclopedias?") The idea is to use the other person's own words against him so that you can get some kind of commitment.

Here's a news flash: Embarrassing people isn't the best way to initiate a business relationship.

Never try to stuff a contact's words down his throat. No matter how creative your argument, no matter how pristine your logic, no matter how right you are, you won't build rapport, and you won't build a business relationship with the person. By the way, here's an alternative response to "I'm not interested" that is about a thousand times more effective than quoting the person's words like a prosecuting attorney:

Salesperson: I'd like to meet with you so I can show you . . .

Decision-Maker: I'm really not interested in talking about any of that with you.

Salesperson: You know, I have to tell you, that's exactly what XYZ Company said when I first called them. That was before they saw how much time on the assembly line we could save them with our widget program. I'd love to show you the plan we put together for them— why don't we get together this Tuesday at 10:00?

THE REALITY: Polarizing the conversation doesn't help you turn around objections.

Myth #14:

The Customer Is Your Enemy

"Use whatever information you have about the buyer against him when you go in for the kill."
—Closing advice heard from a sales "expert"

THE MYTH: You can succeed in sales by launching a series of psychological attacks based on defining your customer as the opponent—and by developing a "battle plan" based on your customer's perceived weaknesses. It's us against them!

There are countless variations on the terrible advice you may get on how to intimidate your way to sales success. In our book, for instance, the supposed "expert" breaks his "opponent" into various demographic and ethnic categories. He then shows you how to intimidate your "opponent" by using closing tricks designed for specific racial, age-related, and social groups!

Are you dealing with elderly "opponents"? Then here's your battle plan: Speak very slowly, charm the pants off of your enemy, then issue clear instructions. That's all there is to it.

What if your "opponent" is a young couple? In that case, you should issue plenty of authoritative instructions, turn the couple into "impulse buyers" by appealing to their pride, and close, close, close.

Middle-aged customers? Play to the opponent's vanity by treating him as younger than he really is, issue plenty of compliments, then go in for the kill.

I wish I could tell you that the advice on manipulation and intimidation stopped there, but the advice only gets worse. If you're dealing with a Jewish buyer, we are told, you should keep it brief and use only "low-key" pressure (but pressure, nonetheless!). Is it possible one could, over the course of time, encounter Jewish people whose objectives or goals are worthy of discussion? Apparently not.

How about Hispanic buyers? There's equally simple advice for selling to them. Get the "opponent's" entire family involved, be aware of his or her religious predispositions, and make the buyer believe you're trying to get the best possible price for the group. Close the family as a whole, and you're in business. This advice, apparently, is meant to be applied to those of Costa Rican, Cuban, Venezuelan, Argentinean, Mexican, Puerto Rican, Ecuadorian, and Dominican descent; the same principles are (supposedly) valid for all of these groups and any others who boast a Spanish-speaking heritage. What could be simpler? (Suppose one is dealing with a person of Hispanic heritage whose family lives in another city? What is the closer supposed to do? Fly out to meet the family?)

How about Asians? Well, you'll be pleased to learn that a similarly straightforward set of principles applies to potential customers from Korea. Or the Philippines. Or Japan. Or China. Or the Pacific Islands. All of these groups of "opponents," apparently, operate under exactly the same mindset. Keep your sales presentation slow for them. Display sincerity. (Don't actually be sincere with Asian "opponents," of course—just display sincerity.) Appeal to the bottom line, then close by appealing to the value you mean to deliver. Again, you shouldn't bother building your discussions around what the person is trying to accomplish. Doing so, apparently, is not a good investment of your time.

Do you have a prospective African-American customer? In this case, you must remember that your younger "opponent" is very likely to be an impulse buyer, and so you should be very emotional in your close and emphasize "showmanship." You must also bear in mind, apparently, that this "opponent" is more likely to buy because of your own personality than because of the reputation of your company. Older African-American "opponents," on the other hand, "tend to have total trust in most people." (Colin Powell? J. C. Watts? Vernon Jordan?) If we want them to buy from us, we should be sure to keep their financing agreements "uncomplicated" so we can then use appropriate closing strategies that will make them "willing to buy."

What a load of nonsense. This kind of advice for intimidating or tricking various ethnic or age groups into buying is at least half a century old; it was always shamefully discriminatory; it always said more about the salesperson than it did about his or her prospects. Unless you feel like resurrecting the worst stereotypes of the first half of the twentieth century, you should treat your prospective customer as an individual and ask intelligent questions about what he or she is trying to do.

THE REALITY: Treat prospects as individuals. Don't intimidate them or make the mistake of assuming that you can use the same overaggressive strategies for members of a given group.

MYTH #15:

You Can "Convince" People to Buy from You

"Convince him to buy based on the value you add."
—Advice a major software firm offered its sales
representatives in a recent training presentation

THE MYTH: Selling means convincing.

Recently, salespeople at a major software firm were instructed to find the highest-ranking decision-maker they possibly could, reduce the perceived risk of buying their product, and then "get him to do the things necessary for the project to succeed."

If only we could!

Selling is not a matter of convincing other people to do what we want. It's a matter of putting together a proposal that makes so much sense to them that *they decide to buy from us.*

People buy for their reasons, not for ours. We can't really get people to do the things that we want them to do, and we certainly can't convince them to buy based on the value we add. What we can do, however, is take the time to identify exactly how they define value, and develop a recommendation that's closely aligned to that definition. This is a process that usually takes much more time than the typical salesperson is willing to commit.

We have a saying at my company: 90 percent of the sales that fail after we make a formal recommendation fail *because we didn't gather the right information*. And I really believe that that's true.

Take a moment right now and think about the last 10 or 12 times that you took the time to develop a formal recommendation for a prospect.

I'm not talking about the times someone called you up and said, "Hey, do you handle widgets?" Nor am I talking about the times when you called someone up and got a more-or-less instantaneous "yes" decision within a few days of making contact. I'm talking about those situations where you were in the running for a deal, but you were competing with someone else. I'm talking about the situations where you had to put together a formal presentation that would be evaluated critically against those of other suppliers.

In those situations, when you didn't get the business, why do you think you didn't get it?

Is it possible that the people you were competing with knew more about what the person was trying to accomplish than you did?

We would argue that, in most cases, that's exactly why you didn't get the business. The competition put together a plan that made more sense to the prospect. In all likelihood, they simply asked better questions than you did. After all, there are hundreds, or even thousands, of potential plans that we could recommend to a given prospect. But there's only one that will truly make enough sense to that prospect for him or her to buy.

To get the deal, we have to recommend the right plan—the plan that makes sense. To identify the plan that makes sense, we have to ask the person the right kinds of questions.

Effective selling is asking people what they do, how they do it, where they do it, who they do it with, and why they do it that way . . . and then helping them to do it better. In fact, this is how we define effective selling. In our model, 75 percent of the sale is completed *before* the presentation. We spend the vast majority of our time gathering information. Then we say, "Makes sense to me . . . what do you think?"

The way most people sell is based on trying to convince the person to buy—before any meaningful information has been gathered! When the sale closes . . . it's a coincidence. And more often than not, this kind of closing relies on "tricks" that people believe will somehow convince the other person to overlook his or her misgivings.

THE REALITY: Forget about trying to "convince" the prospect to do anything.

MYTH #16:

Sales Is a Numbers Game

"It's all numbers."
—Perennial sales maxim

THE MYTH: Make a million calls, or send a million e-mails, and you'll be successful.

Contrary to popular opinion, sales is not simply a numbers game. It is, more accurately, a ratios game. In other words, sales is an *intelligent* numbers game.

The other day, I happened to come across an Internet "marketing opportunity" on the World Wide Web; its name was very similar to that of one of the companies we train, and the search engine I was using pointed me toward the wrong site. This site urged those who stumbled by to join its program. The objective: sell directory listings to "one of the fastest-growing Internet business opportunities ever conceived." (That sounds suspicious enough to begin with.)

Anyway, the site basically promised its readers

that, simply by sending out enough e-mails, they could rise to the highest level of the professional salesperson—because "sales is a numbers game."

This is a very misleading statement—so misleading that it qualifies as a myth.

Sales efficiency can actually be measured in three basic categories. They are:

- Total first appointments
- Ability to close the deal
- Ability to negotiate the best deal

Why those three? Because, if you think about it, if you're making the right number of appointments, if you're putting together the right presentations that turn into sales, and if you're negotiating for the best value, then you're going to hit your sales targets. The prospecting doesn't exist in a vacuum.

When we do our programs, one of the questions we'll ask people is—"How many sales calls do you make a day?" They'll give us all kinds of answers. Sometimes, a person will say, "eight." And we'll say, "Great—why that number?" And the salesperson never knows what to say to that. The point is, you have to select a number that makes sense in terms of your own personal selling ratios. You can't work in a vacuum.

Everything is interconnected. A low daily calling number is obviously going to affect the total number of deals we close. And a low number of total deals will affect our negotiation, because if we're always behind quota, we're not going to be negotiating from a position of strength.

In fact, our skill level in *all three* of these areas will affect our overall performance.

In our training programs, we ask people, "How many ways could you possibly double your income as a salesperson?"

They come up with a lot of answers, but they usually don't get the *right* answer, which is that there are only five ways.

Think about it. If you wanted to double or improve your income, there's only five ways to do it:

1. You could simply dial twice as many people. (For most people, that's not an option.)
2. You could improve your dials to contacts ratio. (If you could double this, without changing anything else, you would double your business.)
3. You could improve your contacts to appointments ratio. (Same thing. If you improved this ratio by practicing better turnarounds—which we teach people how to do—and if everything else remained constant, you'd double your income.)
4. You could improve your appointments to

sales ratio. (If you improved your sales skills and kept everything else constant, you'd see an increase. Theoretically, if you improved your skills so much that you closed twice as many sales, you'd double your income.)

5. Or, finally, you could sell deeper into the account or alter your pricing structure. (By offering more products/services, you could sell twice as much.)

That's it—those are really the only five ways you could double your income.

I hope you can see now that selling isn't really a numbers game—it's more of a ratios game. It's understanding and taking control of the way these numbers work together. Just focusing on the front end—the initial appointments—doesn't give you the whole picture, and it doesn't help you improve your skills in presentation or closing or negotiation.

THE REALITY: Don't just focus on the raw numbers—focus on the ratios.

Myth #17:

Stare 'em Down

"Mind game warfare."
— A sales "expert's" description
of the presentation process

THE MYTH: Win the argument and you'll win the sale.

Some people think that selling is a numbers game (see Myth #16), and focus obsessively on the prospecting end, leaving their other skills undeveloped or underdeveloped. There's a related and equally dangerous myth that selling depends, first and foremost, on a supercharged, prerehearsed presentation.

At my company, we call this kind of selling "low-information" selling because it's knee-jerk, superficial selling based on few, if any, questions. It's based on the assumption that, by overcoming every logical reason that the other person can throw our way, we can somehow create the desire to buy what we have to offer. When someone says, "Well, we've got X with our current supplier," the salesperson says, instantly, "We've got X, too!" Wham! It's a little bit like a shot in hockey, it's so quick. Some salespeople think that if they only play the game quickly enough, they can *make* the other person decide to buy.

I've actually read a book that told salespeople to make their prerehearsed presentation, "overcome" all the "objections," deliver some aggressive rhetorical closing technique, and then *stare* at the prospect while silently repeating the words "Buy it, buy it, buy it, buy it." As though repeating some internal sales mantra could make the person give you a positive response! What nonsense.

In this type of selling, there's very little meaningful information being gathered. Immediately after asking a few superficial questions (if, indeed, there are any questions at all), the salesperson says, "Let me tell you all about what we do." Then he spreads a brochure out on the table and executes what we call a "product dump." (This is also known as "throwing up" on the prospect.)

The salesperson spends a great deal of time going back and forth between getting the information and making a new presentation. When the plan makes sense, it's a coincidence.

In this selling model, the presentation is not based on unique information. And, of course, to close the sale, people usually try to use closing tricks, like the ones we discussed in Myth #2.

Now, does that kind of closing technique ever

work? Sure—one-third of the time, anything works!

Let me explain what I mean by that.

We sell one-third of our prospects simply because we connect with the right person at the right time. Maybe the company is in active search mode and under some kind of time pressure; maybe we got the person on a good day. But we make these sales simply because we call or show up; virtually nothing we do (short of outright incompetence) is likely to lose the sale for us.

The second third of possible sales is very different. We don't get that third because of factors we can't control: the pricing, the relationship the customer has with the competition, or because of other factors. Someone else showed up before we did, and that business is not available to us. These are opportunities that we just can't depend on turning into sales. As I said, about one-third of all our prospects eventually fall into this category.

The final third is where we can really separate ourselves from the pack. That's the third where our actions make a significant difference. If we make a commitment to continuously improve our selling routine, to improve our own skill base, to increase our own capacities and refine and upgrade our goals, then we can close more of these "up for grab" sales.

So—slapshot selling does work *some* of the time. But it can only deliver sales you were going to get anyway.

Slapshot selling is the exact opposite of the way we advise people to try to sell. It's low-information selling.

In the most effective selling model (which is very different from the "low-information" selling model), 75 percent of the sale is completed *before* the presentation.

You understand why, don't you? Because people make the decision to buy for *their* reasons, not for our reasons. We have to obtain a great deal of information to find the "do" that enables us to present, not just any plan, but the *right* plan—the plan that really does make sense to the other person. We have to gather the right information, then *verify* our information, so we match our recommendation to the unique reason for buying that matches up seamlessly with what *this* prospect is doing.

Once we know what the other person actually does, we're in a better position to use our presentation skills. But *without* that knowledge, presentation skills don't really mean very much. And they certainly can't "make" the other person buy from us.

THE REALITY: Skip the "stare 'em down" approach—and spend most of your time in the information-gathering phase.

MYTH #18:

The Quicker You Make a Recommendation, the Better

"Speed kills."—Highway warning

THE MYTH: You should take any available opportunity to close the sale.

After you've made some kind of initial contact, some sales gurus would have you believe you should, as soon as possible, try to make a recommendation and close the sale.

The truth, I am here to tell you, is a little more complex.

There are, to be sure, some situations when you can expect to close the sale during the first meeting or discussion. There are also, however, a good many situations where you can expect to conduct two or three meetings before you receive a yes or no answer. The key to success lies in understanding your sales process—rather than attempting to push it forward to presentation from the first moments of the relationship.

When we talk about "the sales process," we're really talking about our ability to withhold our plan or proposal until we know for certain that we have enough information to develop a truly customized proposal.

You remember from the previous chapter, I hope, that most of our work in sales should come during the information-gathering phase. In fact, 75 percent of our work should come *before* we make a recommendation.

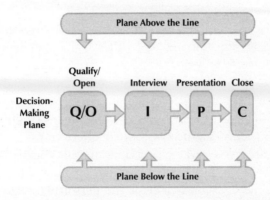

In gathering customer information, we don't want to sound like we are simply marching lock-step through a prewritten list of questions. Instead, we want to engage the prospect in an honest-to-goodness conversation about what he or she does. (Fortunately, people love talking about this topic!) As we follow the other person's conversational lead and pose appropriate "do"-based questions, we want to be aware that there are a number of forces affecting the person we're talking to.

These forces are part of what we call the "decision-making plane." Within this plane there are influences at work above and below.

Above the plane, your prospect/decision-makers could be dealing with various issues for which he or she is responsible to customers or others in the organization, such as an imminent merger with another company, personnel issues, budget challenges, a new product launch, and so on.

Below the plane, there are likely to be issues involving subordinates and other team members that range from personal goals to parking spaces, from motivation to major redesigns of an internal Web site. We must recognize that all these factors exist, uncover them during the information gathering process, and deal with them effectively.

Before you make a presentation, ask yourself: Am I sure I'm talking to the right person? (This is either the decision-maker or the person who can get the decision made for you.) If the answer is no—you are not ready to make a formal presentation.

Ask yourself: Am I sure this plan makes sense, based on what I know this person is actually trying to do? If the answer is no—you are not ready to make a formal presentation.

Ask yourself: Have I discussed all the budget issues with my contact? Does the pricing make sense? (Raise the issue yourself—don't wait for the prospect to do so.) If the answer is no—you are not ready to make a formal presentation.

Ask yourself: Have I established a realistic timetable? (If the implementation or delivery schedule is still theoretical, there's a problem.) If the answer is no—you are not ready to make a formal presentation.

Ask yourself: Does my contact know I expect to close this sale? (If you have any doubt, say something like this: "I'm going to gather everything we've done into a formal proposal for our meeting next Tuesday, and at that point, I don't see any reason why we wouldn't be able to finalize this." See what happens!) If the contact does not know that you plan to close the sale, then you are not ready to make a formal presentation.

After all, what makes more sense—delivering five customized proposals to five prospects who really are "playing ball" with you—or delivering 25 uncustomized proposals that have little or nothing to do with what people are trying to accomplish?

THE REALITY: You'll close more sales by withholding your proposal until you've gathered all the relevant information.

MYTH #19:

People Need You

"Constantly probe to uncover the need."
— Online sales advice on how to conduct a meeting

THE MYTH: You can "build the need" through close questioning of the prospect.

Here's an excerpt from a telesales script someone asked us to critique recently. (The script was developed by a sales manager at a mortgage refinancing company.)

> Mr./s. _____, when was the last time you evaluated your overall interest-bearing debts, including the interest you pay out each month on your home, to determine whether you can lower your monthly and annual spending that will increase your overall cash flow?

> Mr./s._____, if you could save thousands of dollars on the interest you pay on

your mortgage while saving hundreds, if not thousands, of dollars on your other high interest debts and you were able to write it off and lower your tax liability each year, how important would that be to you?

Can you see the problem with beginning a sales conversation with questions like these? (Besides the twisted syntax and longwinded structure, I mean.) The problem I have with these questions is that they're all built on the assumption that the other person *already understands and needs* what we have to offer.

It's as though we imagine the other person is just waiting to hear from us, so he can answer all these intricate questions. These openings are all structured from the salesperson's point of view, which means they address issues that are important to the person placing the call. Because they deal with what the *salesperson* considers to be the prospect's "need," I call them examples of "need-based" selling. (In fact, the script placed all these questions under the heading "Building the Need.")

Is the person really going to remember all the details of when he last evaluated his overall interest-bearing debts? If so, is he going to want to tell us about that evaluation?

Is the person really likely to open up and have a long discussion with us about how important the prospect of saving thousands of dollars of interest would or wouldn't be to him?

If a total stranger called you up on the phone and started trying to "build your need" by asking questions like these, what would you do? My guess is that you wouldn't share that much meaningful information. Your first instinct would probably be to get off the phone as quickly as possible.

That's not how we want people to respond, is it?

Instead of asking people questions based on what we think they need, we should consider asking them about what they've recently *done*. We should consider building our first question around the other person's actions and objectives. We call these kinds of questions "do-based" questions.

Here's a three-step process for building a tele-sales call around a "do-based" question.

- Step One: Open the call. Say the other person's name.

  "Hello, Mr. Jones."

- Step Two: Identify yourself and your company. Give a very brief summary of who you are and what you do.

  "This is Jane Rodriguez from Lone Star Finance. I'm not sure whether you've heard of us, but we've been helping people in the Smallville area reduce their monthly debt payments since 1991."

• Step Three: Pose a question about what the other person does.

  "Mr./s. _____, I'm just curious—about how much would you say you're spending every month in credit card and other loan repayments?"

  Then stop talking. The person either will give you a response about what he or she is doing, or won't. Even if you get a negative response to turn around, however, you'll be in a better position than you would be if you asked questions designed to "build the need."

  Why? Because you'll be looking at the situation from the other person's point of view . . . and asking questions about his world, rather than yours.

  ———————

  THE REALITY: Focus on the "do," not on what you think the "need" is.

MYTH #20:

Slumps Are Inevitable

"Bad luck is part of this job."
—Salesperson explaining a poor month

THE MYTH: Sales slumps come with the job of selling.

Many of the salespeople I meet with tell me things like:

"I'm just going through a down period. It happens to me all the time."

"It's a bad month. I'm used to them. Things always turn around—then there will be another bad month to deal with."

"You've got to take the bad months with the good months, right?"

Are ups and downs in the sales cycle really inevitable? Do we have to have a good month, followed by a bad month, followed by a good month?

To answer this question, we have to realize that

there is a ratio of "no" answers to "yes" answers. A typical sales ratio would look like this: 20:5:1.

What does that mean? Typically, it means you are going to make 20 calls, speak to 5 people, and set up 1 appointment. Or, from another level, it might mean you are going to see 20 people, make 5 presentations, and make 1 sale. Both of those sets of numbers are valid, in our experience.

What is important to understand about that 20, 5, and 1 ratio is that in the process of doing that, you are going to hear the word "no" 19 times. In other words, for every appointment or sale you get, you really do have to collect 19 "no" answers.

Here's the point: We have to learn to count the "no" answers! What's more, we have to learn not to take "no" personally.

Salespeople often create peaks and valleys. They don't replenish prospects soon enough. They have highs and lows because they work their way through their prospects. They make their four or five sales out of the 20 prospects that they had, without replenishing that base of prospects.

Let's look at the process in detail to see exactly how this works.

Salespeople talk about the "big sale" all the time. They say, "Hey, I had the greatest month I ever had last month." We ask them, "What did you do the month before?" "Well, it wasn't so good." "What are you doing the month after?" "It doesn't look so good."

To really understand how well their sales are going, they need to average their sales over that three-month period. When they do, their sales numbers usually look like the average month or worse. The only way around this is to continuously work on developing new prospects and replenish your prospect base intelligently.

Think about the ratio we just discussed. Think about the number of no's you get in relation to each sale. You realize that when you make a sale, you actually lose prospects!

Let's say for argument's sake that you are working on 20 prospects. There are 20 people that you've met once, and you're going back to meet them a second or third time. They are working with you. And let's say your closing ratio is 1 out of 5.

When you make a sale within that group of 20, what actually happens?

Well, you've made one sale and four people have said no. That's one sale out of five prospects, which means that you now only have 15 prospects, (even though 19 still seem to be active). Now if you make another sale from these 15 prospects, you'll only have 10 prospects left. If you make another sale you'll have five prospects left. Soon enough, you'll realize that you actually have nothing left—because you'll be facing an income crisis! You'll realize that there are no prospects to turn into sales!

How long does that take? Depending on your sales cycle, it could be 8, 10, or 12 weeks, 90 days, or it could be a year. Whatever the time frame, your process demands that whenever you get a big sale (or even a little one), you have to check for peaks and valleys and replenish your prospect base. If you don't do that—if you wait until it's obvious that you've worked your way down to zero prospects—you'll have to prospect like crazy to make up for lost time . . . and you'll start the whole stressful process all over again.

That's the ups-and-downs, peaks and valleys pattern. It's not inevitable. Your actions determine whether or not you will experience it.

In order to avoid these peaks and valleys we have to replenish or re-establish that base constantly. If it takes you five "live" prospects to close a sale, you must restock your prospect base with five new "live" prospects immediately after closing a sale. Not one prospect . . . five prospects! (No one, after all, has a closing ratio of one to one . . . although a great many salespeople act as though they do.)

THE REALITY: Replenish your prospect base according to your closing ratio . . . and you'll make sales slumps a thing of the past.

MYTH #21:

Go It Alone

"The salesman is the great American myth of good hope and bad faith. He presents the central promise of capitalism—happiness through material wealth— but is himself on the edges of society, an affable but untrustworthy loner . . . "

—Lloyd Rose

THE MYTH: Asking for help is a sign of weakness.

Many salespeople assume that it's a sign of weakness to bring a manager or other high official in on a sales call. Nothing could be further from the truth!

Talk to your boss about the possibility of working together on key sales. Use the opportunity to get together with your boss as the reason for a second or subsequent meeting with a major prospect. This will give you another tool you can use at the end of a meeting to win a Next Step: "You know what I'd like to do? I'd like to bring my boss in here to meet you next Tuesday at 2:00. He'd be able to give you a lot more background on the program we're talking about. Can we meet then?"

We've trained hundreds of thousands of salespeople to get their manager, their CEO, or some other senior executive to call prospects who are "on the fence" to say something like this: "I understand we're going to be working together!" The reaction is immediate: If a deal is there, the contact will agree. If there's an obstacle, the contact will say exactly what it is. (This explanation, usually more detailed than what the representative would hear directly, often leads to a Next Step involving the manager, the prospect, and the salesperson—a meeting that might otherwise never have happened!)

Don't be hesitant about asking for this kind of help. Your sales manager will almost certainly be eager to work with you to help you close more sales. After all, getting you more commission income is part of your boss's job description!

You can also use technical experts and other team members to move the sale forward.

Use the opportunity to put your prospect in front of a programmer, Web designer, writer, graphic artist, or other key player. This, too, is a great reason to get a commitment for a second or subsequent meeting!

Win action from an on-the-fence prospect by building a meeting with your "expert" into your request for a Next Step. It might sound like this: "You know what we ought to do? We ought to get our technical team together with your technical team. Why don't we try for a meeting here next Tuesday at 10:00?"

You can even use this idea as part of your "makes sense" closing attempt! For instance: "It makes sense to me to get our senior writer on site and begin customization so we can begin the program on the fifteenth of next month. What do you think?"

Always be on the lookout for reasons to have new meetings with new people within the target organization. Use your colleagues and superiors as reasons to set a new meeting, conference, or presentation. Use the team as a whole to formalize forward movement in the sale. You'll close more sales than you will if you simply "go it alone."

THE REALITY: The best salespeople know when to ask for help from other team members.

MYTH #22:

Everyone's a Prospect

"I've got more leads than I know what to do with."
—Salesperson about to have a bad quarter

THE MYTH: A prospect is . . . pretty much anybody.

One of the most dangerous "self-perpetuating" sales myths salespeople tell themselves is that *everyone* they discuss doing business with is a prospect.

As I hope you've gathered by now, I have a very narrow definition of the word "prospect." For me, a prospect is someone who is actively and knowingly moving through the sales process with me—and doing so within my average sales cycle. If the person I'm dealing with doesn't *know* that we're talking about the possibility of doing business together, and doesn't set a Next Step with me that matches the time frame of my average sale, I don't consider the person a prospect.

This narrow definition of the word "prospect"

means that *most* of the people I call and ask to meet with me *do not* become prospects. Yet somehow salespeople ignore this. They assume that each and every phone contact, each and every person who passes along a business card, each and every referral with whom they leave a voice-mail message, is an active prospect. And they treat all of their contacts more or less equally. The myth that everyone is a prospect keeps salespeople from using their most precious resource—their time— intelligently. Instead of reaching out to develop brand-new relationships, they invest their time with people who have proven, by their actions, that they are not interested in becoming prospects!

Imagine that you have a ball, and that every time you call someone up on the phone and ask for an appointment, you are throwing that ball out to the person you just connected with on the phone. In other words, each time you use your approach to ask a new contact to schedule an appointment with you, what you'll really be saying is this: "I am looking for someone to play ball with me."

If the ball comes back—in the form of a Next Step from your contact—then you have a prospect.

If the ball doesn't come back—then you don't have a prospect. I never cease to be amazed at the number of people I train who seem to think that a prospect can be someone who *doesn't* throw the ball back. These people forget that there are many, many ways for someone to say "no"—and that most of those ways don't actually use the word "no." They use words like "I'll think about it" or "Let me talk about it with my boss" or "Call me next week sometime when things aren't so busy."

Most salespeople buy into the myth that you are a prospect by default. The truth is that people *aren't* prospects until they prove by some kind of action that they want to move through the sales process with you. Yet every day, across America, salespeople keep calling and calling, waiting to hear the actual word "no!" They fixate on four or five people for a whole week, usually people who haven't thrown back the ball by agreeing to sit down for a meeting.

The vast majority of the people salespeople talk to during the course of the sales day are, in fact, opportunities for future business, not prospects.

Opportunities may also be known as candidates, suspects, fallbacks, or leads. Whatever you call them, they're people we have not yet gotten to "play ball" with us. The single biggest reason for performance problems in the world of sales, in my opinion, is that salespeople treat opportunities (people who aren't "playing ball") just like prospects (people who are).

So—how do you develop the right number of relationships with actual prospects?

Fortunately, intelligent daily cold calling habits can help you connect with the right number of new contacts each and every day. You can set your own daily prospecting quota—and use your telephone and a sound calling script (see Myth #6) to hit that quota.

Eventually, it all comes down to dials. A dial is simply an attempt to reach a *new* contact—someone you haven't spoken to this week—by phone in the hopes of generating revenue for yourself and your company. The question is, how many dials do you need to make each day? Typically, we find that when people set a goal of between 15 and 20 dials per day, practice their calling script, and hit the dialing target, they generate about one new appointment per day.

So set a goal of, say, 20 dials a day—and then set an appointment with yourself. Write the time down. Block it out in your datebook or Palm Pilot. It's very important to take this kind of formal scheduling step. I tell salespeople that the most important sales appointment they can schedule on any given day is with themselves. It's the appointment they allot roughly one hour each and every working day to making prospecting calls to potential new customers. Prepare a *printed* lead list with all the contact names and phone numbers you will need ahead of time; do not "conduct research" as you go along.

Assuming that you sell by means of face-to-face meetings, you should keep the call brief and focused closely on the date and time you want to get together with the person you're calling. *Do not attempt to sell over the phone*. (Unless, of course, you are working in a telemarketing environment in which your aim is to close over the phone.)

For most salespeople, the development of *real* sales prospects, new people who are willing to meet face-to-face to discuss the possibility of working together, should be *your first priority*. I strongly suggest that you devote part of every selling day to this activity, and that you never, ever miss that appointment you schedule with yourself. It is, quite simply, the most important appointment of any selling day. That one daily appointment is all you need to ensure that you spend your time with real prospects . . . not imaginary ones.

THE REALITY: Not everyone you have a discussion with is a prospect. Only those people who make a commitment to take some kind of action within a specified time frame should be considered prospects.

MYTH #23:

Fast Talk Carries the Day

"The ability to think on one's feet."
— From a job description for a salesperson

THE MYTH: Improvising in response to big questions always wins sales.

Recently, I was on a sales appointment with one of our salespeople. The prospect asked, "Why should I buy from you?" In response, my salesperson went off on a long tangent about our company's history, our guiding philosophy, our most recent successes, and so on.

In other words, he was winging it. He was making up a long answer to a very short, very direct, and very predictable question.

Now, this question—"Why should I buy from you?"—is one of those questions a good professional salesperson should be able to answer from a sound sleep, with little or no variation. The answer should sound something like this:

"Well, let me tell you why XYZ Company decided to buy from us. They were impressed that our core concepts had already been field-tested with over half a million salespeople around the world. They liked our reinforcement plan. And they liked the fact that we were able to tailor our program to an extremely complex market for them. Finally, they liked the fact that we had a bestselling book that they could use as supplementary material for their people. That's why they decided to go with us—and why they're one of our repeat customers."

When my salesperson paused to take a breath, I said my piece, offering the concise summary I just shared with you. We eventually got the deal.

When it comes to answering the big questions—questions like, "Why should we work with you?"—winging it is not your best plan. You *must* be ready with a confident response. One of the most effective responses you can make to these kinds of questions is to share why key customers decided to work with you. This is a much, much better approach than improvising at length.

You should have a clear understanding of exactly why your company's #1 account decided to buy from you . . . and, for that matter, how the sale took place. It doesn't matter whether you made the sale or not—find out what went into that decision from someone who can give you all the details. (If your sales manager doesn't know, consider asking the CEO or president of your organization. You'll be surprised at the detailed answer you receive.)

We have a saying at our company: *People communicate through stories.* This is definitely a story you should be able to tell concisely, powerfully, with enthusiasm, and in basically the same way, time after time. Right now, there is a company that brings your organization X thousand dollars per year. What was the starting point of that business relationship? If you have to improvise the answer, you're in trouble.

In any situation—and particularly in response to the question, "Why should I buy from you?"— you should be ready to explain precisely why ABC Company, your biggest customer, bought from you.

On a related note, you should also prepare a list of references that your prospect can contact at any time. Make certain the references are solid and will speak highly of your organization. If your references are respected within the industry, their endorsements can carry a lot of weight—and perhaps even clinch the sale for you.

THE REALITY: Slow down . . . and be prepared to explain, in detail, why your #1 account bought from your company.

The "Killer Question" Overcomes Any Objection

"What do I have to do to get you into a Yugo today?"
—Plaintive wail of an (now-unemployed) auto salesman

THE MYTH: The use of the most tiresome question in sales is defensible in any situation.

You've heard the "killer question" before. You know what it sounds like. We all know what it sounds like. It's some variation on, "What do I have to do to get you to . . . " (fill in the blank).

Poor salespeople think this "killer question" is the best way to circumvent resistance from prospects. In fact, it's the best way to broadcast the fact that you haven't done your job as a salesperson.

Let me share a story that will illustrate exactly what I mean. A few years back, Bill, one of my employees, received a call from one of those companies that sells expensive carpet cleaners—you know, the kind that hotels use. Their goal was to sell these machines to homeowners. The salesperson called Bill at home, introduced himself, and asked whether Bill wished his carpet was cleaner.

Bill said, "Sure."

Then the salesperson asked if Bill was interested in a "free carpet cleaning."

Bill said, "Sure."

The salesperson suggested a time that he could drop by. He asked whether Bill and his wife would both be in at that time.

Bill said, "Sure."

The fateful day rolled around. The salesperson arrived on schedule. Bill let him in, shook his hand, and thanked him for coming by. They walked into the living room. Bill showed him the carpet. The salesperson asked, "Can you show me where I'd plug in the machine?"

Bill said, "Sure." And showed him where to plug in the machine.

The salesperson plugged in the machine.

Bill started to walk away. The salesperson called him back to the living room. "Wait a minute," the salesperson said. "I have to give a presentation to you and your wife."

Bill said, "Oh. I didn't know that." (There was no reason for Bill to know that. The salesperson had never mentioned it. As far as Bill was concerned, there was some carpet-cleaning service that had called hoping to show him what a great job it could do.)

Bill dutifully called his wife, who came into the

room. The three sat down together and the salesperson delivered his presentation. The husband and wife nodded attentively at all the key points. Then the salesperson dismissed them, cleaned the carpet, and summoned them back again in about 15 minutes.

"Well," the salesperson said, "what do you think? Does it look cleaner than you've ever seen it before?"

Bill said, "Sure."

"Does this look like the kind of carpet you'd like to come home to every night?"

Bill said, "Sure."

The salesperson smiled. "Well, then," he said, "why don't you give it a try?"

Bill said, "Give what a try?"

The salesperson said, "Our carpet cleaner. Why don't you give our carpet cleaner a try?"

Bill looked confused. He stared at the floor for a minute, then he said, "But you've already cleaned the carpet."

The salesperson said, "No, I mean, why don't you give it a try as in *buy* it, keep it for 30 days, and if you're not absolutely satisfied with it after that point, you can return it for a full refund."

Bill stared at the salesperson for a long moment and said, "I really don't think we're interested."

The salesperson went back and forth with Bill in this way for about 10 minutes. He tried every fancy closing trick he could think of, but all he could manage to get out of Bill was some variation on "We're not interested" or "Why don't you let me think about it." Sensing that there might well be a problem with this sale, the salesperson called headquarters and got his manager on the line. The manager asked to speak to Bill directly.

The manager asked Bill, "Did you like the way the machine performs?"

Bill said, "Sure."

Then the manager asked, "Don't you think the carpet looks great now?"

Bill said, "Sure."

Having established "rapport" with these two penetrating questions, the manager pulled out the heavy artillery.

"Bill—let me ask you something, as one man to another. What do I have to do to get you to buy from us today?"

The manager delivered the "killer question" with all the power, enthusiasm, and assertiveness that one associates with the so-called "master closer."

But it didn't make a bit of difference.

Bill said, "Actually, there's nothing you can do. We're just not buying a carpet cleaner." And he hung up the phone.

The problem with the "killer question"— "What do I have to do to get you to buy from us today?"—is that it assumes that people will answer it by obediently providing a list of "objections" that the salesperson can then "overcome," or even a list of preconditions for buying. These are usually totally unrealistic expectations. Think about it: The salesperson had *completely* mismanaged the sales process. *When he answered the door that afternoon, Bill had no idea that he was going to be given a presentation meant to sell him a carpet cleaner!*

Would you like to know what happens before I go out on a meeting at which I expect to close a sale? During the *previous* meeting or conversation, I'll say something like this: "You know, based on what you've told me today, here's what I want to do. I want to go to my office and look at the scheduling questions you've raised and talk to some of our trainers about the best way to present this program. Then I want to come back here next Tuesday at 2:00 and show you what we've come up with. At that point, I have to tell you, I'm thinking we'll probably decide to set the dates and get started developing the materials. How does that sound?"

In other words, by the time I use my "closing technique"—which is, as you recall, "Makes sense to me, what do you think?"—the prospect *already knows* that I intend to close the sale. It doesn't come as a surprise. If it *does* come as a surprise . . . I'm in trouble!

One of the questions I ask salespeople all the time is: "What do you think is going to happen next in this sale?" They'll give me some answer or other, based on their intuition or their "gut feeling." Then I'll ask, "Now, what does the *prospect* think is going to happen next in this sale?" The difference between the answer to the first question and the answer to the second question is often significant.

The "killer question" is what salespeople ask when they have no idea what the prospect thinks about what they're proposing. Believe me, if the prospect doesn't know he's about to buy from you, asking the "killer question" won't make things any more certain.

Selling isn't a matter of asking magic questions. It isn't a matter of pronouncing the right words. It's a matter of working through the process of slowly making a decision *with* the prospect.

If you stop and think about it, I think you'll agree with me that this really is the only intelligent way to try to sell. What's the alternative? Showing up to talk to someone who thinks you've volunteered to clean his carpet? Asking him what you have to do to get him to buy?

THE REALITY: Don't even think about using the "killer question." It will only send signals of desperation and poor preparation to your prospect.

MYTH #25:

"I Know Everything I Need to Know"

"I know I'm supposed to know something about you by now. But I don't know what it is. I know I was supposed to ask you what it was that I was supposed to know about you by now, and I also know that a) you were supposed to tell me and b) I'm supposed to know it by heart by now. Now, it's not like I don't know anything about you. I know a lot of things about you, and I'm actually pretty sure that I must know something about you that's probably pretty similar to what I'm actually supposed to have asked you about. The only problem is, I don't know what it is. What I do know for sure is that if I let anyone know that I don't know the thing I'm supposed to know about you by now, then everyone will know that I forgot to ask you about it back when I was first supposed to ask you about it. So will you just do me a favor and tell me what the heck it is I was supposed to ask you about . . . without letting anybody know that you're letting me know that?"

—Internal monologue of an unprepared salesperson

THE MYTH: We know "enough" about our best prospects to close the deal.

One of the most dangerous sales myths of them all—and the one I'd like you to bear in mind whenever you think you're "heading for the finish line" with any prospect—is the myth that you "already know" enough to close the sale. Enough about your leads . . . enough about your prospects . . . enough about customers . . . enough about anybody in your contact base to finalize the deal.

Anyone who has ever lost a sale that seemed "certain" can tell you of the folly of imagining that you know all there is to know about an organization or an individual who is considering working with you.

Selling is an *endless* process of asking questions, identifying opportunities, and learning about changes in the other person's situation. Since the realities our prospects and customers face change constantly, our obligation to ask intelligent questions about what's going on in their lives never concludes.

Whenever we imagine that a lead who operates in such-and-such an industry is "just like" a lead who operates in the same industry . . . or that a prospect with a certain goal is "just like" a prospect with a similar goal . . . or that the problems a customer faces today are "just like" the problems he or

she faced last year, last quarter, or even last week
. . . then we've got a problem.

This is, in large measure, a problem of our own
making. It's a problem that sometimes arises out of
good (not bad) selling habits. One of the things we
train salespeople to do, and one of the things I've
asked you to do in Myth #23, is to memorize a
number of success stories related to your company's successful relationships with its customers.
Success stories are an excellent tool for drawing
out points of commonality with your prospect, and
for learning more about his or her unique environment. Success stories become a selling *obstacle,*
however, if they become our *only* means of evaluating the prospect's world. Do you see the difference? If we pass along a success story in order to
get the other person to tell us the details about his
or her unique situation, we've succeeded. If we
pass along a success story in order to get the other
person to agree that we've *already* got the right
solution, without any further information gathering or customization, then we've failed.

How much do you really know about your #1
prospect? When did you last learn something new
from him or her?

These are extremely important questions. If
you've convinced yourself that your relationship
with this person is "so good" that you don't have
to bother asking yourself how much you really
know about this person's situation . . . if you've

convinced yourself that your initial meetings went "so well" that you don't have to find out what is different in your prospect's life this week . . . if you've convinced yourself, in short, that you know everything there is to know about this person . . . then you aren't really doing your job.

If a prospect isn't giving you new information *throughout the sales process*, there really is a problem . . . because effective selling is based on asking people what they *do*. The best definition of selling, as you've learned, is rooted in finding out what the other person does . . . and then helping him or her do that better. This happens by means of a series of mutually agreed-upon Next Steps.

Never forget: Prospects are people who are "playing ball with you" to move the sales process forward . . . so you can learn what they *do*, and then help them *do* that better.

So: A "prospect" who refuses (for instance) to return phone calls is not really a prospect. On the other hand, someone who has agreed to meet with you next Tuesday at 2:00 to see a revised proposal *is* a prospect.

Look at it again: Someone who has met with you once and has declined your request for a future meeting, asking that you call back "sometime next quarter," is *not* a prospect. Someone who has met with you once and asked you to meet with the boss to go over some ideas about how you could work together, *is* a prospect.

These are both fairly straightforward examples. They're fairly easy to understand. But remember our definition: "Prospects are people who are 'playing ball with you' to move the sales process forward . . . so you can learn what they *do*, and then help them *do* that better." This means that *when the learning stops, the relationship is no longer moving forward.* In other words, the person can stop "playing ball" with you simply because *you stop* trying to find out what's new in the other person's world.

So: A person with whom you have a meeting, and who gives you superb, meaningful information—information that helps you to develop a highly targeted proposal or recommendation—is certainly a prospect. But if you go three weeks without calling that same person to find out what's new in his or her world, the fact that you passed along a superior proposal two weeks ago is meaningless. The person is no longer a prospect. You haven't learned anything new *recently*. You've fallen prey to the myth that you "already know" all you need to know.

This is why we must *never* stop asking ourselves how much we know about (for instance) our #1 prospect . . . and *never* stop asking *when* we last learned something new about that person. In fact, there are at least 12 questions that we should be able to answer about what our #1 prospect *does* and how we can help the person *do* that better.

(In reality, of course, there are hundreds of questions you could formulate to match individual situations that connect with individual prospects, but these 12 are a good starting point for developing such customized questions.)

The following 12 questions are the best antidote to the "I know everything I need to know" myth that I've been able to come up with:

- If you cannot answer even *one* of these questions about the contact you currently consider to be your #1 prospect, you've got some work to do with that person. (Moving on is a *good* outcome—it means you have the opportunity to develop new contacts.)
- If you cannot answer *any* of these questions about the person you believe to be your #1 prospect, you are deluding yourself. This person is probably not a prospect at all. Move on! Develop a new prospect!
- If you cannot answer *any* of these questions about *any* of your prospects, the odds are good that you are not gathering the right information during your calls and visits; you should consider changing your interviewing and meeting routine.*

---

* It's also possible that you are simply not reaching out to enough new people in the first place, and spending too much of your time with a very small number of people who aren't providing you with any kind of meaningful information.

1. How did the person you're talking to get this position?

Specifically, when did he or she start working for the company? Do you know? If you asked, do you remember what the answer is?

Ask:

- "Just out of curiosity . . . how does someone become a (job title)?"
- "How did you get this job?"
- "What did you do before you came here?"

At the outset of any meeting with a prospect or customer, it's absolutely essential to remember that effective interviewing must be *focused on the other person's experiences and interests.*

2. What does this person actually do?

How much real authority does he or she have? What kind of access can this person give you within the target organization? If you can't give a convincing, detailed answer to your sales manager's question, "What does the person actually have to do with us getting the business?", guess what? You have more interviewing work to do.

Here's how most salespeople will try to find out what the contact's role is: They'll ask, "Hey, what's your role in all this?" Or: "Who's going to be in charge of such-and-such an area?" The problem with that kind of question is that, if you ask it very early on in the relationship, you're not likely to get a completely accurate response. (See question #3 below.)

One good way to get a sense of what is the person's role in the organization is to ask an appropriate follow-up question about the person's career. For instance: "Did you get promoted into this position, or were you recruited from outside?" (The implication that your contact might have been recruited probably won't hurt your rapport with the contact.) You can follow up with, "When did that happen?" You can also ask, "When did you become responsible for . . . ?" (And here you would name some element of the person's current job.)

3. Will this person be the one making the final decision about whether or not to use your product or service?

Contrary to popular belief, you won't get the right answer if you come out and ask this question directly during the first visit. Instead, ask:

- "What made you decide to do so-and-so?"
- "How did you choose XYZ Vendor?"
- "Who else did you look at/consider giving this job to the last time around?"
- "Why them?"

Don't ask: "Are you the decision-maker?" Early on in the relationship, you are likely to get a misleading (or, let's face it, completely false) answer to this question. The reason? *The length of your relationship determines the quality of your information.* In other words, someone who's sitting down with you for the second or third time is more likely to share confidences with you than someone you've just met 10 seconds ago.

And yet, your job is to determine, from the earliest meeting possible, where the likely zones of influence are within the target company. In other words, you're looking for someone who can move the process forward for you.

If you ask, "How/why did you decide to do such-and-such?" you're more likely to get an anecdote that offers you something resembling the truth about how the company actually went about purchasing products or services like yours the last time around. If the person admits he or she *doesn't know* how the company decided to do it the last time, you must try to arrange a meeting with the person who *does* know the answer to your question. That's more likely to be the person who controls budgets, timetables, and agendas.

4. What's the plan?

What is your prospect's current plan for dealing with the situation you want to help him or her improve? After all, the situation is probably not as new to your contact as it is to you. There must be some kind of plan in place for handling whatever it is that you hope to handle. What is that plan?

If you don't know the answer, consider asking questions like the following: "I'm just curious—as of now, what's your plan for tackling the problem of (increasing sales/reducing downtime/recruiting the right people/whatever)?"

Now stop talking. Listen to whatever answer comes back. Then follow through appropriately on the answer you receive.

5. Why aren't they already using you?

Don't waste your time "probing" for "pain" or "faults" about another vendor. Find out how they made previous decisions, and ask why they aren't using you currently.

When you know the prospect *is* using someone else, and you know the prospect *isn't* using you (even though the current vendor has supposedly made the prospect "unhappy"), *don't* automatically say, "Here's why we're better." Instead, say: "I pulled up my customer list on the computer and I looked for your company, but I saw that you're not one of our customers right now. I'm just curious—why not?"

The answer you get will tell you *exactly* where you stand with this prospect. If the person considered using you in the past, you'll find out about it at this point in the conversation.

6. Who else is the person talking to?

Is the prospect talking to other potential suppliers/vendors? Have you asked? At some point in your conversation—perhaps at the end of the first meeting—you should ask a question that sounds something like this: "I'm just curious . . . who else are you talking to about this?"

If you *know* the person/organization is talking to other people, but don't know which ones, you might try asking, "How did you decide which companies to talk to?" The answer you get to this question and appropriate follow-up questions will not only tell you a lot about your competitors (and perhaps even reveal their identities), but may also help uncover a lot of additional information, including: who else within the organization is involved in making contact with potential vendors, or selecting potential vendors to contact; what the buying criteria are; and what kind of timeline the target organization is working against.

7. What does this individual hope to accomplish?

What, precisely, is your contact hoping to accomplish on an *individual* level? You probably won't learn this on the first meeting, but you should develop a steadily clearer picture of the person's goals. There are plenty of personal goals that can affect the forward motion of a purchase decision; the person you're talking to may eventually choose to share critical information about his or her goals with you—information that he or she might *not* share with colleagues or superiors. For instance: If your contact's personal goal is to get transferred to another division in another city, it's going to be to your advantage to know that.

To find out about individual goals, you can ask questions during one-on-one conversations:

- "How do you like it here?"
- "How would you describe this job?"
- "Just out of curiosity, where do you see yourself going in this job?"
- "What's most important to you here?"
- "What made you decide to stay on in this job?"
- (If you know the contact has family in the area) "Does your family like it here in (city)?"
- "Is this a good place to work?"
- "Based on what you've told me, X seems to be a major priority for you. I'm just curious . . . why?"

Use these kinds of questions to identify what motivates this individual. Is it a promotion? The quest for recognition by the group? The desire to see a son or daughter attend the best private school in the state? Something—perhaps simple force of habit—is inducing this person to get up out of bed each day, fight traffic, and do the job, day in and day out. Use these kinds of questions to get a sense of what that "something" is for this unique person.

8. *What does this company, organization, or work group hope to accomplish?*

How do your prospect's efforts fit into the larger objectives of his or her team or department?

This is an extremely important question. If *you* don't know what the objectives of the group or organization are, you can't build a proposal around those objectives. And if your contact doesn't know what the objectives of the group or organization are, he or she probably isn't the best person to be talking to!

When in doubt, ask your contact questions like these:

- "What are you trying to make happen this month/quarter/year?"
- "How's business?" (The answer to this question will virtually always clue you in to your contact's most important objectives and business challenges . . . assuming, of course, that you're dealing with someone who has some kind of authority and responsibility within the target organization.)
- "How do you maintain a competitive edge in this industry?"
- (If appropriate) "What made you decide to call us?"

Posing questions like these, and developing appropriate follow-up questions, will help to give you a sense of the organization's current situation and critical goals.

9. How does the timeline in this relationship stack up against your actual sales cycle?

How long have you been in discussions with this person? Do you expect the deal to close? If so, when? Does the prospect expect the deal to close at that time, too? How do you know that? Is the period of time between your first meeting and your anticipated closing date longer than, shorter than, or about the same as your real-world sales cycle?

These are difficult questions to ask for most salespeople, but it's absolutely essential that you ask them and determine the no-nonsense answers. If you find, in confronting these questions, that your contact has been stringing you along for 19 weeks, and your actual sales cycle is 10 weeks long, then guess what? This person is not a real prospect. If you find, in confronting these questions, that you have identified someone as a "90 percent" prospect, but now realize that he or she actually has made no commitment to you, has given you no Next Step, and has no date in mind about starting to use what you have to offer, then guess what? This person is not a real prospect.

In order to answer question 9 responsibly, you must keep accurate records. It's not good saying to yourself, "I've been talking to this person for a few weeks now." You must know *how many* weeks, exactly, you have been in discussions with your prospect. Mark your meetings down on your calendar so you have a clear answer to the questions: When was the first meeting? When is it likely (or possible) that this could close? How does that amount of time compare to my average selling cycle?

Remember: Time is vitally important. The longer you exceed your average selling cycle, the LESS likely you are to close the person you're talking to.

10. *What's happening next?*

Throughout the sales process, we must be willing to ask for the Next Step directly. What we say might sound like this:

"I've learned a lot today—what I'd like to do is come back here next Wednesday at 3:00 and bring my boss so you can meet with him. Does that make sense?"

Or it might sound like this:

"You know, based on what you're telling me, I think I should meet with some of your technical people and then come back here next Wednesday at 3:00 to show you what we come up with. Does that make sense?"

Or it might sound like this:

"I really think you ought to hear our president. He's giving a public seminar on the fourteenth of March. Can you make it?"

Or it might sound like this:

"Here's what I want to do. I want to take the notes you've given me today, revise our outline, and come back next week to show you what our full proposal would look like. Can we meet again next Thursday at 2:00?"

Eventually, "what happens next" needs to sound something like this:

"I have to tell you, given everything we've developed here, this really does make sense to me. I think we ought to start on the nineteenth. Does that make sense to you?"

Or perhaps like this:

"You know what I'd like to do? I'd like to get our senior writer in here so he can start talking to your people and developing the materials for the program. That way, we'd be able to hit the launch date you and I had talked about—April nineteenth. Does that make sense?"

Whatever you say, however, you must be able to point to some kind of action that's taking place at a clear, mutually agreed-upon point in the near future. If there is no such action in place, then guess what? You've got nothing.

11. Why does this make sense?

This may be the hardest question we have to ask ourselves about our #1 prospect (or any prospect). *Why*, specifically, would it make sense for this person to decide to work with us?

Or, to put it another way: *Why* is this person currently pursuing the possibility of a business relationship with us?

You cannot answer this question unless you have at least an initial sense of what the person is trying to *do*. When in doubt, focus on . . . What the person is *doing*, has *done*, and is planning to *do* in the future . . . and *how* and *why*.

For instance:

- "What have you *done* in the past to increase your market share?"
- "*How* are you planning to increase market share over the next quarter?"
- "*Why* did you choose that approach?"

Remember: The prospect must never feel as though he or she is being subjected to a list of pre-determined questions. Once you begin the meeting, be sure the conversation flows naturally. Ask about what the person is *doing*—and what he or she hopes to *do* in the future. Ask *how* and *why*.

Many people treat selling as though it were something that's very complex. Actually, selling is simply a matter of finding out what the person is currently doing and why it makes sense to do it that way, sharing your organization's relevant success stories, and finding out whether you can help the person do what he or she currently does better. But as I hope you can see by this point, this is an ongoing process. It's not something that takes place at the beginning of the first meeting and then stops. It's something that takes place throughout the life of your business relationship with the other person.

Sometimes salespeople say to me, "Okay, Steve—I've got it. I have to ask questions and make absolutely sure that I can never know it all. But how will I know when a given proposal or recommendation really does make sense to the other person?"

The answer to this question is actually very simple. If the prospect begins to act as though closing the sale is as important to him or her as it is to you . . . then you'll know that the idea you're discussing makes sense!

THE REALITY: You never know "enough."

APPENDIX

The Myths—and the Realities

MYTH #1: "Always Be Closing"
REALITY: Steer clear of the "Always Be Closing" selling philosophy.

MYTH #2: Selling Requires "Can't-Miss" Closing Tricks
REALITY: Don't bother trying to memorize "can't miss" closing tricks.

MYTH #3: You Can "Warm Up" Your Cold Call with Mysterious Packages
REALITY: Don't risk sending the wrong message by sending a mysterious package.

MYTH #4: Sending Strange Business Letters Works
REALITY: Save the fake money for your next game of Monopoly.

MYTH #5: People Love It When You Pretend You're Not a Salesperson
REALITY: Tell the truth. It's easier to remember.

MYTH #6: Decision-Makers Adore Unannounced Visitors
REALITY: Call first.

MYTH #7: Price Always Carries the Day
REALITY: Build relationships—not just discounts.

MYTH #8: Selling Effectively Means "Trapping" the Prospect
REALITY: Do the homework. Talk to your colleagues. Talk to your supervisor. Get the details about when, where, and how your company has added value. Be ready to share those details when the opportunity arises. And forget about trying to "trap" the prospect.

MYTH #9: Never Ask a Question When You Don't Know What the Answer Will Be
REALITY: Ask prospects big questions and follow the answers wherever they go.

MYTH #10: Always Try to Outsmart the Buyer
REALITY: Don't try to outsmart your prospects and customers.

MYTH #11: Long, Detailed, and/or Wacky Voice-Mail Messages Are Great Selling Weapons
REALITY: Keep voice-mail messages short, sweet, and to the point.

MYTH #12: E-Mail Is Replacing the Telephone as a Sales Tool
REALITY: Use e-mail appropriately—and don't rely on it as a prospecting tool.

MYTH #13: Fight, Fight, Fight When You Hear Negative Responses!
REALITY: Polarizing the conversation doesn't help you turn around objections.

MYTH #14: The Customer Is Your Enemy
REALITY: Treat prospects as individuals. Don't intimidate them or make the mistake of assuming that you can use the same overaggressive strategies for members of a given group.

MYTH #15: You Can "Convince" People to Buy from You
REALITY: Forget about trying to "convince" the prospect to do anything.

MYTH #16: Sales Is a Numbers Game
REALITY: Don't just focus on the raw numbers— focus on the ratios.

MYTH #17: Stare 'em Down
REALITY: Skip the "stare 'em down" approach— and spend most of your time in the information-gathering phase.

MYTH #18: The Quicker You Make a Recommendation, the Better
REALITY: You'll close more sales by withholding your proposal until you've gathered all the relevant information.

MYTH #19: People Need You
REALITY: Focus on the "do," not on what you think the "need" is.

MYTH #20: Slumps Are Inevitable
REALITY: Replenish your prospect base according to your closing ratio . . . and you'll make sales slumps a thing of the past.

MYTH #21: Go It Alone
REALITY: The best salespeople know when to ask for help from other team members.

MYTH #22: Everyone's a Prospect
REALITY: Not everyone you have a discussion with is a prospect. Only those people who make a commitment to take some kind of action within a specified time frame should be considered prospects.

MYTH #23: Fast Talk Carries the Day
REALITY: Slow down . . . and be prepared to explain, in detail, why your #1 account bought from your company.

MYTH #24: The "Killer Question" Overcomes Any Objection
REALITY: Don't even think about using the "killer question." It will only send signals of desperation and poor preparation to your prospect.

MYTH #25: "I Know Everything I Need to Know"
REALITY: You never know "enough."

Cold Calling Techniques (That Really Work!), Fifth Edition

In today's changing marketplace, smart salespeople know that cold calling is more than just picking up the phone—and great salespeople know that the secret to success is technique. Featuring updated information about the newest technology trends, this title offers simple, effective solutions to a challenge all sales representatives face.

ISBN: 1-58062-856-7, Trade paperback, $9.95 ($15.95 CAN)

Closing Techniques (That Really Work!), Second Edition

"Closing the sale" is the part of the job nearly every salesperson dreads, yet it can actually be the easiest part of the sales cycle. Sales trainer Stephan Schiffman shows how to integrate the closing process into a productive, professional sales cycle—and turn prospects into allies, not adversaries. He focuses on helping, not pressuring the customer. His innovative system makes manipulative tricks and high-pressure techniques obsolete.

ISBN: 1-58062-172-4, Trade paperback, $8.95, ($12.95 CAN)

The Consultant's Handbook, Second Edition

The Consultant's Handbook is the definitive resource for those who want to enter one of today's most exciting, challenging, and potentially lucrative fields—consulting. It provides an authoritative, balanced appraisal of the benefits as well as the pitfalls you can expect to encounter in this dynamic field.

ISBN: 1-58062-441-3, Trade paperback, $12.95 ($18.95 CAN)

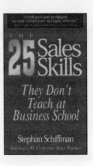

About the Author

Stephan Schiffman is president of D.E.I. Management Group, Inc., one of the largest sales training companies in the United States. He is the author of a number of bestselling books including: *Cold Calling Techniques (That Really Work!), Power Sales Presentations, The 25 Most Common Sales Mistakes, The 25 Habits of Highly Successful Salespeople, Asking Questions, Winning Sales, Make It Happen Before Lunch, 25 Sales Skills They Don't Teach at Business School,* and most recently, *Stephan Schiffman's Telesales.* Schiffman's articles have appeared in *The Wall Street Journal, The New York Times,* and *INC. Magazine.* He has also appeared as a guest on CNBC's *Minding Your Business, How to Succeed in Business,* and *Smart Money.* For more information about Schiffman and D.E.I. Management, please call (800) 224-2140, e-mail *contactus@dei-sales.com,* or visit *www.dei-sales.com.*